PRAIS
The Altar of His Presence

Studies and surveys have shown Christians do not live like they say they believe. Discipleship deficiencies among Christians are prevalent and alarming. Why? Many Christ-followers believe that to be a disciple, they must concentrate on knowing (a rational theology) and doing (a behavioral theology). While both are very necessary, they are not transformative.

The ultimate goal of discipleship is Christ-likeness. What must occur is a relational experience that begins with *loving God* and *loving others*. More human effort is not needed but rather an extraordinary ability provided only by the power of the Holy Spirit.

In his new book, *The Altar of His Presence*, Robert Stone provides a pattern and a process to establish a growing, intimate relationship with God by experiencing His Presence. He gives a historical view of the importance of the altar as well as a practical way to way to establish a personal altar. This book will assist in fulfilling the desire to practice God's Presence. *"And we all, who with unveiled faces contemplate the Lord's glory, are being transformed into his image with ever-increasing glory, which comes from the Lord, who is the Spirit"* (2 Cor. 3:18 NIV).

REVEREND ALTON GARRISON
Assistant General Superintendent
The General Council of the Assemblies of God
Springfield, Missouri

Many people today are often intimidated by the idea of developing a personal and intimate relationship with the Lord. A relationship within which one can actually experience His Presence and recognize His voice as He speaks in many different ways. Robert Stone skillfully opens Scripture to reveal that this idea is actually God's. Furthermore, as God's invitation to us becomes our priority we discover God's purpose, pattern, and pathway to know and experience Him in a new and very intimate way. I highly recommend this book both as a study guide and a daily devotion to discover the beauty of God's Presence more fully. It will truly alter your life.

CHARLES PATTERSON
Pastor Emeritus, Church of the Hills
Charles Patterson Ministries, Austin, Texas

I would personally encourage every serious man of God to get a copy of this ever inspiring devotional book. I can promise that you will be blessed each time you read through it.

BISHOP MCOWEN ANDREW S. MWALE
Senior Pastor, Katawa Jerusalem Temple, Mzuzu, Malawi
Former Division Director, Northern Region
of the Malawi Assemblies of God

The Altar of His Presence is not for those who wish to be motivated by other people's stories. Instead, Robert Stone skillfully weaves life lessons of his own, richly seasoned with Scripture, in order to lead the reader into an altar'ed life.

This devotional will help you to understand and establish your "trysting place"—an appointed time and place to call upon the Lord and to become His voice in our world. May each of us "fully commit to hearing the voice of the Spirit and obeying the illumination He gives from His Word" as we become altar'ed by His Presence in our lives.

RIC SHIELDS
President, Doorways
Broken Arrow, Oklahoma

Prayer is the power that sustains change, drives commitment, and creates the Christ-likeness for every Christian. Robert Stone has laid out the process, potential, and practice of prayer for the believer using systematic and biblically based principles in a devotional form. Follow these principles through study and reflection in each chapter and find a whole new way to experience Christ and the dynamic of the Holy Spirit with life changing results.

DOYLE FULKES
Superintendent, Southern Idaho Ministry Network
of the Assemblies of God
Nampa, Idaho

In writing *The Altar of His Presence,* Robert Stone has put biblical truth at our fingertips. In doing so, Robert has encouraged us to settle in and get to know God in a deep and profound way. He teaches us that by spending time in deliberation and reflection we come to know God and see things in the Scriptures that we might have otherwise missed. By embracing such knowledge, we are able to imprint what we have learned in our hearts and minds, develop spiritual wisdom, and move further along in our walk with God. This is a valuable read for all Christians.

Fran Bates
Mary Kay Independent Beauty Consultant
Austin, Texas

While reading *The Altar of His Presence* I was reminded of an incident that happened several years ago. At that time, I had a nephew who was in special need of prayer. He asked me to pray over him, so we knelt down beside his bed and prayed. Prior to that night I had sought to be filled with the Holy Spirit but had never felt like the work was accomplished in my life. But as we prayed together that night I felt God flooding me with the Holy Spirit; I prayed like I had never prayed before and experienced speaking in tongues for the first time. I now understand what truly happened that night. My nephew and I built an altar and the Lord met us there.

The Altar of His Presence is one of the best books I have read. The book is full of insight born out of Robert's research. He presents it in a very understandable way. The information about the materials and manner of how the people in the Bible built historical altars fascinated me. I was inspired to learn how God blessed every one of His people who came to the altar and that He gave many of them a special ability to communicate with Him and other believers. The book also reminds the reader that an altar can be built anywhere and at any time. The promise of God is true. If we will come to the altar, the Lord will always meet us there.

Finally, in reading this book my spiritual eyes were opened to many things concerning the Holy Spirit's ministry and His ministry at the altar. Anyone who chooses to do so can build an altar and enter the Presence of God in their prayer closet or when sitting on a chair, kneeling before their bed, or even lying down on the living room couch. The Lord wants to meet with each of us during a church service or even in our own backyard. Any place will work. We must decide in our heart to meet with God, and if we will begin with thanksgiving and praise the Spirit will manifest His Presence. I encourage everyone to read this book with an open heart. I can promise that by doing so they will find that it is not important where we build an "altar" and that by doing so they will be positioned to receive the best of blessings from Him—His Presence.

Dwight Karm
Retired Owner, Paramount Insurance Repair Service, Houston, Texas

Robert Stone is a revolutionary. In his new book, *The Altar of His Presence*, Robert gives insight to mankind's ability to commune with God on a personal and unprecedented level. Robert can take the most difficult biblical concepts, particularly involving the wonderful intervening Presence of the Holy Spirit, and make them seem extraordinarily simple for the average Christian. Robert's teaching that each of us can experience the manifest Presence of God through a loving relationship with our Lord is truly life-altering. I encourage everyone to join the Lord at the altar of His Presence (the meeting place of our heart). Thank you, Robert, for another "altar'ed" work. Your message has forever changed my view of the Holy Spirit and His work in my life.

JEFF KNEBEL
Brushy Creek Community of
Austin Christian Fellowship
Austin, Texas

The Altar of His Presence is a powerful, passionate, and uplifting read that inspires the reader to come experience the manifest Presence of God. This book is rich with spiritual guidance, biblical truth, and practical application. Robert leads us through a journey into the proper order of God and His will for our lives. The book details God's promise to meet us, deliver us, heal us, and create in us a new heart and mind. All we have to do is believe!

Author Robert Stone uses Scripture, stories, and vivid word pictures to wonderfully illustrate how much God loves us and wants to bless us with a personal relationship with Him. This book is motivating, captivating, encouraging, and invigorating. Finally, *The Altar of His Presence* reminds us that through God's grace we not only have a place, a person, and a people to meet the Lord, but most importantly we have God in us, and that is where God ultimately wants to meet. There's no better time than now!

MICHAEL VALITON
Pastor of Finance and Operations, Lake Hills Church
Austin, Texas

Robert Stone has struck the perfect combination of biblical history and practical daily living application with his new book, *The Altar of His Presence*. I love how each chapter opens with a new focus on the ministry of the altar. The organization of the material will remind the reader of the importance of having a personal relationship and approach to God the Father through daily communion. This study guide will give the reader a fresh, new way of approaching the altar of God while bringing clarity and focus to their faith.

RYAN HORN
Surprise, Arizona

Thank you for allowing the Holy Spirit to speak through you in your most recent book, *The Altar of His Presence*. It is a timely message in the hour we now live and minister in.

As I read your book, I kept thinking about the church culture that has developed over the past several years. The altar is seldom mentioned and is being emphasized less and less. Truly if we are going to live an altar'ed life we must recognize the importance of having a personal, enduring relationship with our Lord and Savior, Jesus Christ. We must contend for a relationship that embraces meeting with Him and coming to Him on a continual basis.

Robert Stone, I know your book *The Altar of His Presence* is going to make an impact on all who read it. Those who have an ear to hear what the Spirit is saying will greatly glean from its truths you have so divinely written. Thank you for allowing me the privilege and honor to be one of the first to read *The Altar of His Presence* and to be blessed and enlightened by it. May God richly bless you for your obedience in writing such a profound book.

HAROLD and MARILYN MORTON
Senior Pastors, Word of Life World Outreach
Conroe, Texas

The Bible tells us in Romans 12:1 that our reasonable service unto God is to present our bodies as a living sacrifice, holy and acceptable for the Lord.

In his new book, Robert Stone shares great insight and fresh revelation concerning the work of the Holy Spirit at the altar. His insight and understanding on the manner in which the men of God in the Bible constructed, worshiped at, and encouraged others reveals how the ministry at the altar is to be used, the purpose of the altar, and how each and every one of us can build one. Robert shows that the altar is essential and indispensable in our relationship with God, a connecting place between God and His people and the gate into His Presence. I highly recommend this book and will surely use it to teach my congregation.

PASTOR ARNO BOËTIUS
Tabernacle of David, Aruba

The Altar of His Presence is no mere devotional but a sacred journey. Fasten your seat belt and prepare to have your life totally altar'ed!

DARYL MOCZYGEMBA, Austin, Texas

This book is a must read for those who want to be informed about those in the history of God's Word and who have experienced not only the move of God in their life but how the same should be happening in our lives, the complete church. One paragraph says it best—our "altar'ed way of life" must break out of the four walls of the modern church and into the lives of others. We must speak out of who we are in Christ Jesus, not just what we have learned. We must walk in the newness of the ascended life. We have been planted together in the likeness of His death, raised in the likeness of His resurrection, and seated with Him far above all principalities and powers.

The reflections and space for our own responses from each chapter ask the reader to listen to the Holy Spirit for a heartfelt response to what God has shown to them personally. The essence of *The Altar of His Presence* is best stated in section eight, "The marks of an altar'ed life are consistency, faithfulness, and stability." The fire that originally came from above must never go out on the altar (or in our spiritual lives). Take time to fan the flame. Ask the Lord to help you see from His perspective as you worship and adore His holy Name.

DEAN and JANET WILSON
Dean Wilson Ministries, Denton, Texas

The Altar of His Presence is a must read for every Christian! Robert's devotional study not only opened my understanding, but every time I would read a new section my spirit would leap inside of me. I found myself both excited and overwhelmed by the Lord's Presence many times. If you are seeking to have fresh outlook on the Holy Spirit's ministry, this is the book for you. It will bring heaven to earth and the glory of God will flood your heart and soul.

TONY and BECKY GARRIFFO
Owners of EnGedi Pest Control, Waller, Texas

Are you hungering for more of God's Presence in your life? Do you long for God to meet you in your quiet times? Are you seeking His face wholeheartedly? Robert's new book, *The Altar of His Presence*, will point you to a life that presses in to the Lord and His Spirit. If you accept this invitation, you will behold the glory of God and be transformed forever!

LYNN MCGOLDRICK
Bible study teacher and small group leader
Austin, Texas

DESTINY IMAGE BOOKS BY ROBERT STONE

Gifts from the Ascended Christ

THE ALTAR
OF HIS
PRESENCE

◆

INSPIRING INTIMATE ENCOUNTERS WITH
THE GLORY OF GOD

ROBERT STONE

DESTINY IMAGE® PUBLISHERS, INC.
P.O. Box 310, Shippensburg, PA 17257-0310
"Promoting Inspired Lives."

This book and all other Destiny Image and Destiny Image Fiction books are available at Christian bookstores and distributors worldwide.

Cover design by Eileen Rockwell
Interior design by Terry Clifton

For more information on foreign distributors, call 717-532-3040.
Reach us on the Internet: www.destinyimage.com.

ISBN HC: 978-0-7684-1556-8
ISBN LP: 978-0-7684-1557-5
ISBN 13 TP: 978-0-7684-1226-0
ISBN 13 eBook: 978-0-7684-1227-7

For Worldwide Distribution, Printed in the U.S.A.
1 2 3 4 5 6 7 8 / 21 20 19 18 17

This book is dedicated to those throughout my life who taught me the wonder of meeting the Lord at the altar, which resulted in my learning to live the altar'ed life. Using their example, the Holy Spirit captured my heart's attention and filled me with a hunger and thirst for living in my Lord's manifested Presence.

ACKNOWLEDGMENTS

I want to thank my parents, Wayne and Yvonne Stone, for their dedication to the Lord Jesus Christ and their example of how to live the altar'ed life.

I also want to thank my wife, Susan, for her dedication and agreement that together we would live a life in the altar of His Presence.

Together with my parents and my wife, I have spent thousands of hours of enjoyment worshiping and praying with people of like precious faith.

I have encountered, entered, and enjoyed being in the secret place of the Most High God, which has enabled me to expose tens of thousands of people to the way of the altar'ed life.

I also want to honor some of the wonderful people who inspired me to live the altar'ed life.

That list would include Pastor and Mrs. E.R. Roberts, Pastor Clifford Barnes, Dr. Stan Toler, Dr. Opal Reddin, Dr. Kelley Varner, Dr. Clarice Fluitt, Elnora Overton, Dr. Robert Cornwall, Dean and Janet Wilson, Richard and Mary Bennett, Dennis Roberts, Pastor and Mrs. Robert Florence, and my wife's parents, Albert and Connie York.

CONTENTS

INTRODUCTION

The Lord God Almighty wants a meeting with you! Yes, you understood me correctly. The Creator of all there is in heaven and earth wants to get-together with you! His heart is filled with the desire to spend time with you as if you were long lost best friends who had found each other after years of separation. Reconnecting with such a friend can be exhilarating partly because of the mystery that comes with the changes the time apart has brought and partly because of the rekindling of fond memories that were thought lost.

Childhood memories generally have a great effect upon our lives. Mine are no exception. I remember my first day at kindergarten, surrendering my life to the Lord, being in my aunt's wedding, and my grandmother's warm peach cobbler.

The memory that stands out is my grandmother's warm peach cobbler. Like most folks, I love peaches and warm peach cobbler. I know what you are thinking. Many people love peaches. But my affinity for peaches may include more than just having an appetite for tree ripened summer fruit. Part of my love may include the sweet summer memories of eating my maternal grandmother's peach cobbler made from peaches grown in my grandfather's tiny orchard. As I remember, the peaches were sweet sweet; and the cobbler? It was amazing. It was especially so when my grandmother would serve me a small bowl of her warm cobbler from the season's first picking.

That memory stirs more memories. Memories such as the peach trees bursting into bloom on a late April morning or my grandmother taking time to pray for the Lord to protect the peaches from a late spring freeze. Included in those memories are the many years I watched my grandfather caring for his little orchard of twenty-three peach trees and one apricot tree as though it was a nursery filled with newborn babes.

I can almost see him carefully inspecting each tree. His experienced eye would search the peaches diligently to see if some insect had invaded the orchard overnight. If he found an insect, I would have to listen to him debate (with himself of course) as to the reason why the insect was able to survive the insecticide he had carefully sprayed a few days before. Upon the end of his morning inspection he would unroll the long orange hose that was kept between the fence and the house. He liked that hose. He believed it was the perfect diameter for watering his precious trees at just the right rate, which was when the spigot had been turned exactly three and one half revolutions open.

When spring turned into summer my grandfather would tie his funny looking old scarecrow up on a pole between the second and third row of trees. I would help him bring the odd looking figure with his old ladder from the garage. Afterward we would string aluminum pie tins above the trees. Both the scarecrow and pie tins were used to keep the starlings and other birds away.

June became July and the nights were warm and humid. Early July mornings were filled with my grandfather adjusting that funny looking scarecrow, tightening up the string on the pie pans, watering the trees or finding a two by four to prop up a limb bending from the weight of the swelling fruit. It was usually around my birthday in late July that my grandmother would make her first ask. She wanted to know if the peaches were about ripe. If grandpa's answer was in the affirmative, my grandmother would respond by taking her annual trip to the cellar.

The cellar was cool and smelled funny. The dusty shelves were filled with empty mason jars used the previous year. They needed to be sterilized before we could start picking the now soft, swollen fruit. I still remember grandpa bringing one of those softened peaches into the kitchen for us to taste. Every year, the first peach brought great delight. I remember, more times than I can count, putting a piece of peach into my mouth and the juice dribbling out from the corner causing us all to giggle. I would wipe my chin with my small hand. Even now, I can almost feel the stickiness of that juice on my chin and the back of my hand. The joy of harvest time arriving and the season's first warm peach cobbler are a defined picture in my mind's eye. It is a picture I can't forget.

But as wonderful as those memories are, my fondest memories are my meetings as a young child with the Lord.

I know meetings can be intimidating. A call from the principal's office or the IRS can bring a lump to anyone's throat. But meeting with the Lord is different. There is no hidden agenda. No judgment is awaiting you. You have already been accepted as righteous because of your confession of faith in Christ Jesus. He's not going to ask for your money or for you go give Him a loan. He owns the cattle on a thousand hills and the hills under the cattle. In fact, the whole earth and all everyone in it belong to Him.

How do I know about such meetings? It is because one of my early memories concerns the person who taught me the importance of meeting with the Lord. His example captured my heart's attention and helped to develop within me a hunger and thirst for living in my Lord's manifested Presence. This person? My dad.

Dad's relationship with the Lord Jesus Christ was founded on the Scripture found in Exodus 30:6:

> Put the altar in front of the curtain that is before the ark of the Testimony—before the atonement cover that is over the Testimony—**where I will meet with you.**

Dad loved meeting with the Lord. In the church I grew up in my dad could be seen sometimes before, always after, and from time to time during a church service kneeling with his handkerchief out, tears flowing down his cheeks with his heart open to God.

Dad saw the altar as his meeting or trysting place. The word *tryst* is an old English word not used much in today's modern society. A trysting place is an appointed meeting place agreed upon by two individuals. It also speaks of a place where intimacy or a tryst occurs (as between special friends or lovers). In a spiritual sense, a trysting place is defined as a secret place, either in time or space, where an individual consistently goes to meet with God.

The psalmist David spoke of such a place in the first verse of the ninety-first Psalm:

> He that dwelleth in the secret place of the most High shall abide under the shadow of the Almighty (KJV).

The Lord Jesus, both by example and by word, taught His disciples the importance of entering into that special place with God. Mark 1:35 says, "Very early in the morning, while it was still dark, Jesus got up, left the house and went off to a solitary place, where he prayed." Our Lord taught His disciples to follow His example during the Sermon on the Mount in Matthew 6:6:

But when you pray, go into your room, close the door and pray to your Father, who is unseen. Then your Father, who sees what is done in secret, will reward you.

My dad dearly loved his special meetings with the Lord Jesus and the Holy Spirit. Whether by himself in the early morning or soon after the evening meal, Dad would gather with my mom and his three boys, either at the end of the couch or in one of the bedrooms. He led us in seeking the face of his Lord and Master. My brothers and I would kneel in front of him and Mom. They would put their hands upon us. Sometimes we would be finished in a few minutes. Other nights we would be there for almost an hour.

Though Dad went home to be with the Lord years ago, I can still hear him pouring out his heart to God. I heard Dad pray thousands of times before he died. His altar time was always filled first with thanksgiving and praise for the Lord and Savior he loved, honored, and adored. Within a minute or two from the start, Dad's voice would break and tears would fill his eyes and begin spilling down his cheeks. Dad's tears were seldom a result of sadness. Sadness held no place with Dad. His brokenness was a result of his having a contrite spirit.

Dad's prayer time wasn't filled with fear or remorse over some terrible secret sin that had infected his life. No, his brokenness came from spending time every day in the manifest Presence of the Holy Spirit. To begin, Dad would recall how his Savior's love had changed his life, his mother's healing of milk fever, and his gratefulness to the Lord for giving him his wife and sons. Decades after his salvation, Dad would consistently thank his Lord for bringing about the circumstances that brought his family to God. His thirst for more of the glory of God was born out of his desire to be filled to overflowing with the righteousness, peace, and joy that only the Spirit of the living God could bring.

It is no wonder that I identified the altar with being in God's Presence. During our nightly prayer meeting I came to understand the need to be filled full of God's grace and glory. It was with Dad in the secret place of the Most High that I was first given experiential knowledge of the Holy Spirit. The development of that knowledge continued to grow because the altar'ed life that began at home was lived at church. What we experienced at church, Dad explained and lived at home. What we experienced at home was discussed at church. Sometimes before or during, but always after, either Mom or Dad would take our hands and lead us to the altar area of the church to pray with them.

Oh, how marvelous and wonderful those times were for me. And, along the way, the altar'ed life became my life. I loved being with Dad, the Lord Jesus, and the Holy Spirit. I don't remember exactly when I understood, but because I was living an altar'ed life my own life was being altered. The Holy Spirit did not teach me to "say my prayers." He taught me to pray in, by, and though Him. I found the joy of being with Him. I found that place in the Spirit that other men such as Tozer, Ravenhill, Bounds, Nelson, and Packer found. Instead of getting religion, I truly found the altar'ed life. I learned the secret to living in the place of the Lord Most High.

By the time I was a teenager I was building my own altar. I found my trysting place. I came to fully know the altar'ed place is not geographical but spiritual. It is not without but within. Spending time in His manifested Presence made me aware of my Lord's heart for the lost. I heard Him calling for laborers to enter into His harvest field, and I responded by telling the Lord I would go. Several times I found myself consumed by His call upon my life. Each time I responded like the prophet Isaiah, "Here I am. Send me." This is the secret of my spiritual life and my ministry. I have never been drunk with wine or any other drink. I have never been high on illicit or prescription drugs. But I have been filled, permeated, saturated, and intoxicated to overflowing with the glorious wonder of the Holy Spirit more times than I can count.

This coming April I will celebrate forty-five years of ministry. Through the years I have tasted and seen the ever growing goodness of the Lord Jesus Christ.

Without hesitation, I can say that living the altar'ed life will alter your life. Like Enoch who walked with God, if you walk with God long enough, God will take you. He will take you places you cannot possibly visit or live without Him.

I can promise you that if you will learn to submit to the Lord Jesus Christ and the Holy Spirit; if you will seek for the Spirit's control of your body and soul; if you will put your all on the altar; you will experience His majesty and glory beyond description. Once you experience the Holy Spirit on that level, you, like Enoch, will find yourself encountering new dimensions of His Presence on a continual basis.

I know. I have found unspeakable joy in His manifested Presence. I have found His illuminating light, His emanating life, and His indescribable love. His Word is alive in me. His peace has broken down every wall. You too can find your trysting place in Christ. He wants to meet with you and show you how to foster His manifested Presence.

Living the altar'ed life will alter your life. I have learned to submit to Him. I seek for His control of my will, my words, and my ways. I have found the joy of abiding in His manifested Presence as well as the joy of His Word being manifested in and through my life. This devotional is about helping you find your trysting place in Christ.

I pray that as you go through the following pages you too will come to the altar of His Presence. I pray that you find your own spiritual trysting place and that you will be filled full of the Holy Spirit.

I believe I have been called and chosen to help you. Call upon the Lord. Seek Him with all of your heart and soul. I promise He will lead you. I promise your journey will be one you would not trade for anything the world has to give. Remember, He wants to meet with you and show you how to abide within His manifested Presence.

MY PRAYER FOR YOU

I pray that as you walk through the pages of this book you will choose the altar'ed life. I pray that you will hunger and thirst for something new, for there you will be filled. You will find your secret place in Him and you will be filled to overflowing with the Holy Spirit and power.

I hope you learn to call upon the Lord and seek Him with all of your heart. I want to impart that which I have received so that you too can be led by the Holy Spirit. I promise if you will build an altar—the Lord will meet you there. The altar'ed life will alter everything about your life. Prepare yourself. Be strong and courageous. You are about to enter the best season of your life.

Therefore, brothers, since we have confidence to enter the Most Holy Place by the blood of Jesus, by a new and living way opened for us through the curtain, that is, his body, and since we have a great priest over the house of God, let us draw near to God with a sincere heart in full assurance of faith, having our hearts sprinkled to cleanse us from a guilty conscience and having our bodies washed with pure water. Let us hold unswervingly to the hope we profess, for he who promised is faithful. And let us consider how we may spur one another on toward love and good deeds. Let us not give up meeting together, as some are in the habit of doing, but let us encourage one another—and all the more as you see the Day approaching (Hebrews 10:19-25).

SECTION ONE

THE ALTAR'ED PROMISE

Put the altar in front of the curtain that is
before the ark of the Testimony—before
the atonement cover that is over the
Testimony—where I will meet with you.
—EXODUS 30:6

1

THE PROMISES ARE YES AND AMEN

For no matter how many promises God has made, they are "Yes" in Christ. And so through him the "Amen" is spoken by us to the glory of God (2 Corinthians 1:20).

We live in a modern world where pledges and promises of men are more likely to be broken than kept. This is in stark contrast to what we see over and over again in the Scriptures. The Scriptures teach us that if God said it—you can count on it. The One True and Living God is entirely and completely faithful to His Word. Because He is faithful, we who are the recipients of His promises can rest with complete assurance that God will fulfill everything He has said. The foundation of our confidence rests on the truth declared by Paul in Titus 1:1-3.

Paul, a servant of God and an apostle of Jesus Christ for the faith of God's elect and the knowledge of the truth that leads to godliness—a faith and knowledge resting on the hope of eternal life, which God, who does not lie, promised before the beginning of time, and at his appointed season he brought his word to light through the preaching entrusted to me by the command of God our Savior.

Such was on the mind of Paul when he reminded the church that every scriptural promise has found its fulfillment in Christ Jesus. Paul had access to the promises found in the Old Testament. This included the promise found in Exodus 30:6. It was no doubt taught to Paul at an early age. But even the teaching of that verse by Gamaliel did not compare to Paul's experience on the Damascus road. That day Paul fully tasted the splendid joy of all he had learned about the Messiah, only found in the Person of the Lord Jesus Christ.

The light of the Master's glory was so bright it blinded him. The voice of the King of Glory was so awesome it changed him.

All of the promises Paul knew were fulfilled in Christ, including the promise we are addressing in this book. This is the promise that says if we are willing to meet with Him at the altar, *He will meet us there* (see Exod. 30:6).

All of the promises of God are yes and amen. Our Lord is a Savior, a Friend, and the Lord of Glory. He wants to meet with us. He wants us to meet with Him. Our coming ignites faith. When we expect, we receive. Whom we seek, we find. When we knock, the door opens. Then faith reaches through the open door and takes hold of what He has promised with the expectation of us finding the fulfillment in Him. The Bible says, "God is not a man, that he should lie, nor a son of man, that he should change his mind. Does he speak and then not act? Does he promise and not fulfill?" (Num. 23:19). The answer is no! All the promises are yes and amen in Christ Jesus.

Pastor Roger Roth said, "Each generation has a distinct mission, but it must expand on the foundation and purpose of the preceding generation." I believe the mission of this generation of Christ followers is to come together to create a spiritual dwelling place where God dwells and where we are actively fostering His Presence. We are more than participants; we are His people. And as His priests, let us be offering up spiritual sacrifices and living as vessels full of the Presence of the living God.

Reflection

> *Then the King will say to those on his right, "**Come**, you who are blessed by my Father; take your inheritance, the kingdom prepared for you since the creation of the world"* (Matthew 25:34).

Response

_____

_____

_____

_____

_____

_____

_____

2

COME TO ME

*Give ear and **come** to me; hear me, that your soul may live.
I will make an everlasting covenant with you, my faithful
love promised to David* (Isaiah 55:3).

Paul calls the future glorious appearing of our great God and
Savior, Jesus Christ, the blessed hope (see Titus 2:13). While we
wait for Him to descend from Heaven with the shouting voice of an
archangel and with the trumpet call of God (see 1 Thess. 4:16), He
desires to come and meet with us today by His Spirit. Open your
heart as you read these words. Hear His voice say:

> ***Come** and see what God has done, how awesome his works
> in man's behalf!* (Psalm 66:5)

> ***Come**, all you who are thirsty, **come** to the waters; and you
> who have no money, **come**, buy and eat! **Come**, buy wine
> and milk without money and without cost* (Isaiah 55:1).

> ***Come**, let us sing for joy to the Lord; let us shout aloud to
> the Rock of our salvation* (Psalm 95:1).

Why does He want us to come? So our soul will live. His idea of life is not existence but abundance. For He said, "I am come that they may have life, and that they may have it more abundantly" (John 10:10 NKJV). The Bible is filled with invitations, exhortations, and commands to come to Him. The idea of coming necessitates movement. To come means to move from where we are to where He is. This calls for us to forget what is behind us and move toward what is ahead. Like pressing toward a goal or prize, we must come toward that which God has called each one of us to in Christ Jesus (see Phil. 3:14).

Each of us is in danger of being infected by the antichrist viruses that are so prevalent in our secular society. The spirit of the world almost chokes us at times. Possessions, power, prestige, and prominence are its symptoms. God's preventive vaccines and healing antibiotics start to take effect with our coming forward into Scripture, prayer, a godly friendship, or a small group of Christ followers. In our coming we are made to feel supreme love for One we have never seen; we find ourselves talking every day to Someone we cannot see and emptying ourselves in order to be full. In our coming, we die so we can live, forsake in order to have, give away so we can keep. We see the invisible, hear the inaudible, and understand that which passes understanding.[1] Hallelujah!

If you will come:

- He will *come* with clouds (Mark 13:26).

- He will *come* as the rain (Hos. 6:3).

- He will *come* as lightning (Matt. 24:27).

- He will *come* as refining fire (Mal. 3:2).

- He will *come* as resurrection power (Phil. 3:20-21).

- He will *come* as the Chief Shepherd (1 Pet. 5:4).

- He will *come* as the Morning Star (Rev. 22:16).

- He will *come* as the King of kings (Matt. 25:31-34).

Reflection

Jesus replied, "If anyone loves me, he will obey my teaching. My Father will love him, and we will come to him and make our home with him" (John 14:23).

Our Lord and Savior is calling us to Him. He has chosen to make us His dwelling place. I ask you to come to Him with your heart. Call upon Him. He is near. He wants to be with you. He will withhold none of Himself, but show you His grace and glory.

Response

NOTE

1. Paraphrased from A.W. Tozer.

3

LET US BOW DOWN AND WORSHIP

Come, let us bow down in worship, let us kneel before the Lord our Maker; for he is our God and we are the people of his pasture, the flock under his care (Psalm 95:6-7).

The Bible contains some very intense and intentional words used to describe the various affections and actions people of faith have employed in their coming to meet with the Lord. These words most always speak of the honor and respect the Hebrew people had for Yahweh. The most common of expressions include "bowing" and "kneeling." The depth of expression with which people of old came before the Lord had much to do with their attitude, respect, and love for the Most High God. We see this in Genesis 18:1-2:

And the Lord appeared unto him [Abraham] in the plains of Mamre: and he sat in the tent door in the heat of the day; and he lifted up his eyes and looked, and, lo, three men stood by him: and when he saw them, he ran to meet them

34

from the tent door, ***and bowed himself toward the ground*** (KJV).

Here Abraham was expressing his profound reverence and humility before the Lord. His expression probably included falling upon his knees, then gradually inclining his body until his forehead touched the ground. In his bowing, he was declaring that Jehovah God, the God Almighty Who is the King of kings and the Lord of lords, was to be honored and be the recipient of his highest reverence and adoration.

In fact, the Hebrew word *shachah,* which is translated as *worship* in Psalm 95:6, means to bow down or to prostrate oneself before the Lord in admiration, honor, and respect.

The instruction of the psalmist shows the prevalence of this posture in prayer as seen when Eleazer, sent to select a wife for his master Isaac, bowed before Yahweh (see Gen. 24:26). Isaiah said "every knee will bow" to God (Isa. 45:23), and the apostle Paul said he bowed his knees to the Father (see Eph. 3:14). This honoring attitude was a common one to Ezekiel and was exhibited by Peter, James, and John on the Mount of Transfiguration (see Ezek. 1:28; 3:23; Matt. 17:6).

> *Let us* ***come*** *before him [His Presence] with thanksgiving and extol him with music and song. For the Lord is the great God, the great King above all gods* (Psalm 95:2-3).

To bow, extol, and worship the Lord shows honor for who He is. Coming to meet with Him is a voluntary act of honor and reverence. By bowing before Him we declare that our relationship with Him is valued above all the people and things in our lives. I remember the worship that poured from the heart of my father. As a boy, I heard over and over again my prostrate father telling his Lord and Savior how much he loved, honored, and adored Him. He taught me that when we worship, we are assigning value to the Lord—valuing Him above all else. Our word *worship* is derived from the old English "worth-ship," which speaks to the value placed on our relationship with the Lord. I urge you to worship and value Him today. There is none who compares with Him. How awesome is our Lord, the Most High!

Reflection

The Lord Jesus is looking for our coming, our bowing, and our worship even when we are facing challenges, trials, and disappointments. Begin a list of the things He has done in your life. Count your blessings and give Him thanks that in spite of all that life can sometimes throw at us, our Lord is great and greatly to be praised.

Response

4

LET US KNEEL BEFORE THE LORD

Therefore God exalted him to the highest place and gave him the name that is above every name, that at the name of Jesus every knee should bow, in heaven and on earth and under the earth, and every tongue confess that Jesus Christ is Lord, to the glory of God the Father (Philippians 2:9-11).

Throughout the Bible, kings, queens, and persons of superior rank were shown honor and respect by people kneeling or bowing before them. Joseph's brothers bowed as they came into his presence (he was serving at the time as an Egyptian of high rank; see Genesis 43:28). David bowed himself three times when he met Jonathan, the son of Saul, Israel's first king (see 1 Sam. 20:41). David's queen, Bathsheba, bowed to King David when she came into his presence on behalf of their son Solomon (see 1 Kings 1:16,31). When coming to ask Elisha to intervene on behalf of her son, the Shunammite woman knelt before the young prophet (see 2 Kings 4:37).

But when it came to the worship of Yahweh, kneeling was both common and consistent (see 2 Chron. 6:13). Josephus, who described Solomon's actions, says that at the conclusion of his prayer Solomon prostrated himself on the ground and continued worshiping for a long time.[1] In spite of the king's edict, Daniel knelt upon his knees and prayed three times a day (see Dan. 6:10). In the New Testament, there are several examples of people kneeling before the Lord Jesus in worship and prayer, including Steven in Acts 7:60, Peter in Acts 9:40, and Paul in Acts 20:36. The best known example is found in Matthew 2:11: "Coming to the house, they saw the child with his mother Mary, and they bowed down and worshiped him. Then they opened their treasures and presented Him with gifts of gold and of incense and of myrrh."

Paul tells us that there is coming a day when every knee will bow and tongue confess that Jesus Christ is Lord. Rather than wait for that day, I encourage you to start today. Come before the Lord in prayer. Build an altar of praise and worship. Kneel before Him. The physical act of kneeling will tell of your love and submission. Such action incites a kind, reverential attitude in spirit, soul, and body. Let your words flow freely from your heart and mouth giving the Lord the honor, glory, adoration, obedience, and service due Him.

The principal New Testament idea here is found fifty-nine times in the Greek word *proskuneo*. The word literally means to "kiss (the hand or the ground) toward." When we kneel or fall prostrate upon the ground, the action precipitates a sense of awe, veneration, and adoration. The Lord Jesus told the Samaritan woman in John 4:23-24, "Yet a time is coming and has now come when the true worshipers will worship the Father in spirit and truth, for they are the kind of worshipers the Father seeks. God is spirit, and his worshipers must worship in spirit and in truth." True worshipers are genuine, without guile or false humility. They worship in spirit and in truth. It is the attitude of the heart that matters. In reality, out of the heart of man, the highest and best part of man, we should be showing purity of expression to the Most High God. All praise and worship should be in harmony with the Holy Spirit who is the Spirit of truth (see Rom. 8:5; John 16:13). Such worshipers the Father is still seeking today.

Reflection

Bow your knee and lift your voice to worship Him. Declare these words: "Hear my heart today—there is none like You my God, there is none like You. You are my everything. You are my all. I bless Your Holy Name. Amen."

Response

NOTE

1. James Orr, Ed., International Standard Bible Encyclopedia, s.v. "Adoration," http://www.studylight.org/encyclopedias/isb/view.cgi?number=223.

5

CALL AND HE WILL ANSWER

This is what the Lord says, he who made the earth, the Lord who formed it and established it—the Lord is his name: "Call to me and I will answer you and tell you great and unsearchable things you do not know" (Jeremiah 33:2-3).

Come...bow...kneel...call. The progression of these terms seems almost childlike in its simplicity. Such were the words of Jesus when He said, "Let the little children come to me, and do not hinder them, for the kingdom of God belongs to such as these" (Mark 10:14). Too often we have been hindered in our coming by the cares of life and the deceitfulness of riches (see Matt. 13:22). Poor time management has hindered us from taking the time to kneel before the Lord our Maker. So we have not called because we were not sure He would answer. But we need to know that the Lord, the One compassionate and gracious God, is slow to anger, abounding in love and faithfulness. He continues to maintain love and is forgiving of wickedness, rebellion, and sin (see Exod. 34:6-7). He loves for us to come to Him, build an altar, and call upon His wonderful Name.

Adam's son Seth also had a son, and he named him Enosh. At that time men began to call on the Name of the Lord (see Gen. 4:26). Enosh in Hebrew is *ar'q' qara'* meaning to call, call out (with the Name of God), and to cry out (for help). It can also mean to utter a loud sound to summon, invite, or call for. Ar'q' qara' is a primitive root with the idea of verbally approaching a person met.[1] The idea is of a child calling out in the night to a father. The concept behind the word is one of prayer, supplication, or appeal. The Bible encourages us to sacrifice thank offerings to God and call upon the Lord in the day of trouble—He will deliver us, and He will honor us (see Ps. 50:14-15).

We often wonder why God has not done anything to change many of the issues in the world. We wonder why God hasn't brought peace to war, overturned abortion laws, stopped the violence in our cities, or brought revival to our land. Many of us are waiting for God to take action when in fact God is waiting for us. God is waiting for His people to *call* upon Him. He is waiting for His followers to genuinely repent of lives that have become too busy, too focused on success, and too measured by how much money we make. He is waiting for us to humble ourselves and return to the altar of His Presence.

The Lord promised Jeremiah that He would answer us and tell us great and unsearchable things we do not know. He also told the prophet that if we would come, call, and pray to Him, He would listen to us and that when we seek Him with all of our heart we will find Him (see Jer. 29:12-13). In his letters to the Christ followers in Rome and Philippi, Paul wrote, "there is no difference between Jew and Gentile—the same Lord is Lord of all and *richly blesses all who call on Him*" (Rom. 10:12) as well as, "Do not be anxious about anything, but in everything, by prayer and petition, with thanksgiving, present your requests to God. And the peace of God, which transcends all understanding, will guard your hearts and your minds in Christ Jesus" (Phil. 4:6-7).

Reflection

For many, the altar'ed life begins like the story of Bartimaeus in Mark's Gospel (see Mark 10:46-52). When the blind beggar realized his opportunity to have a transformed life, he began to call out, "Jesus, Son of David, have mercy on me!" Many rebuked him, but he shouted all the more. He called until his answer came, until he was brought to Jesus, until the Lord opened his eyes to the light, until his life was altar'ed. Don't stop calling. If you will call, He will answer.

Response

_____

_____

_____

_____

_____

_____

_____

_____

NOTE

1. James Strong, *Strong's Exhaustive Concordance of the Bible* (Peabody, MA: Hendrickson, 1987), H7121.

6

WE ARE HIS PEOPLE

Know that the Lord is God. It is he who made us, and we are his; we are his people, the sheep of his pasture (Psalm 100:3).

There is nothing that brings more identifiable misery to a human life than lifeless Christian religion. For the most part, religion is a system of thought, feeling, and action that is shared by a group of people. By its nature the philosophy of any religion, including Christianity, creates an identity for God as well as God's people. Mistakenly, such philosophy seeks to evaluate God and the circumstances of human life from mankind's point of view, which has caused many modern believers to live a self-centered, need-focused, and entertainment-based religious life.

Religion is mankind's way of trying to determine, define, and describe who God is (His identity), what God expects from man (a false identity), and what man should expect from God (false hope).

43

This same religious spirit was seen in the Egyptian and Roman cultures, who worshiped many gods and goddesses, all of whom looked like them. Both of these kingdoms believed that their king (Pharaoh or Caesar) had descended from the gods, making them their god's people.

In contrast to such thinking is 1 Peter 2:9-10, which says:

> *But you are a chosen people, a royal priesthood, a holy nation, a people belonging to God, that you may declare the praises of him who called you out of darkness into his wonderful light. Once you were not a people, but now you are the people of God.*

Do you see the difference? We are chosen (see Eph. 2:22). We are holy and belong to Him. Belonging is not based on what we are, but the Lord Who lives within us.

We are the house, the dwelling place, the habitation of the Lord (see John 15:19). Jesus said He and the Father would live within us (see John 14:23). We also are the temple of the Holy Spirit (see 1 Cor. 6:19). Therefore, the Lord is our hope and the strength because we belong to Him (see Joel 3:16). Our identity is not built on what we know about God but upon God knowing us. We are His. He made us (see Ps. 95:6). He takes great delight in us (see Ps. 149:4). He will never leave or forsake us. He is our helper and we are His people (see Heb. 13:5-6).

As His people, we are the blood relation of spiritual Israel (not the Jewish race) through the new birth (see 1 Pet. 1:23). A people for God's own possession. The idea here is a people over and above all others. Such people are His possession in a special sense (see Eph. 1:14). How is this possible? The church of the Lord Jesus Christ is made of a people He bought with His own blood, making us His possession and flock (see Acts 20:28).[1] What is a reasonable response? To declare, publish, and make known the great goodness of the most mighty God by praising Him, by proclaiming and celebrating His Name Who called us out of darkness into His wonderful light. His wonderful light consists of awe-inspiring simplicity, transparency, and excellence, as well as clarity of virtuous thought and purity of holy expression.[2]

Reflection

*Shout for joy, O heavens; rejoice, O earth; burst into song, O mountains! For the Lord comforts his people and will have compassion on his afflicted ones. But Zion said, "The Lord has forsaken me, the Lord has forgotten me." "Can a mother forget the baby at her breast and have no compassion on the child she has borne? Though she may forget, **I will not forget you***! See, I have engraved you on the palms of my hands; your walls are ever before me" (Isaiah 49:13-16).*

Response

NOTES

1. A.T. Robertson, "Commentary on 1 Peter 2:9," *Robertson's Word Pictures in the New Testament* (Broadman Press 1933; Renewal 1960), http://www.biblestudytools.com/commentaries/robertsons-word-pictures/1-peter/1-peter-2-9.html.

2. Strong, *Strong's Exhaustive Concordance*, G1804, G703.

7

LET US NOT GIVE UP MEETING TOGETHER

Let us not give up meeting together, as some are in the habit of doing, but let us encourage one another—and all the more as you see the Day approaching (Hebrews 10:25).

There is a wonderful and unique revelation found in the New Testament. That is, meeting with Christ Jesus is not only personal (vertically with Him) but also corporate (horizontally with Him through others). The first meeting is direct, the second indirect. The first with the Head, the second with the Body of Christ. The first totally spiritual, the second possibly involving our spirit, soul, and body.

The first is found in Ephesians 1:17:

*I keep asking that the God of our Lord Jesus Christ, the glorious Father, may give you the Spirit of wisdom and revelation, **so that you may know Him better**.*

The second can be seen in Colossians 2:2-3:

*My purpose is that they may be encouraged in heart and united in love, so that they may have the full riches of complete understanding, in order that **they may know the mystery of God, namely, Christ**, in whom are hidden all the treasures of wisdom and knowledge.*

The Hebrews writer is speaking of both when he wrote, "Let us not give up meeting together." While we know from the context that the writer is speaking of meeting together as the Body of Christ, in our prayer meetings with each other we are meeting with Christ Jesus. When we meet with each other, understanding and revelation is given to us of who He is in the lives of others with like precious faith.

We see Him and hear Him by watching and listening to others pray. This is one of the things that was revealed to me many years ago. Kneeling in front of my dad and listening to him pray over me gave me understanding of the way Christ Jesus intercedes for me. For there were times that it wasn't my dad praying for me, but the Christ by Holy Spirit praying through my dad's heart and voice—for me!

And pray in the Spirit on all occasions with all kinds of prayers and requests (Ephesians 6:18).

In the same way, the Spirit helps us in our weakness. We do not know what we ought to pray for, but the Spirit himself intercedes for us with groans that words cannot express. And he who searches our hearts knows the mind of the Spirit, because the Spirit intercedes for the saints in accordance with God's will (Romans 8:26-27).

Praying with dad gave me understanding that the Lord Jesus Christ can be declared and experienced as the Lord and Savior of His people. He is "Wonderful, Counselor, Mighty God, Everlasting Father" (Isa. 9:6), and, "They will come with weeping; they will pray as I bring them back. I will lead them beside streams of water on a level path where they will not stumble, because I am Israel's father, and Ephraim is my firstborn son" (Jer. 31:9).

Reflection

> **Let us draw near to God** with a sincere heart in full assurance of faith, having our hearts sprinkled to cleanse us from a guilty conscience and having our bodies washed with pure water. **Let us hold unswervingly** to the hope we profess, for he who promised is faithful. **And let us consider** how we may spur one another on toward love and good deeds (Hebrews 10:22-24).

Let us pray together with others and not stop meeting with Him.

Response

APPLICATION

If my people, who are called by my name, will humble themselves and pray and seek my face and turn from their wicked ways, then will I hear from heaven and will forgive their sin and will heal their land. Now my eyes will be open and my ears attentive to the prayers offered in this place (2 Chronicles 7:14-15).

I am praying that you have entered into dialogue with the Lord and the Holy Spirit about taking the steps toward the altar of His Presence. If so, you have joined masses of people who are now learning to foster His manifested Presence. You are probably being impacted in marvelous and yet unpredictable ways. It is important for you to seek the Lord with your whole heart and soul so that you can experience His flooding goodness, grace, and glory.

Prepare to make application of His promise.

1. Yes, He has *promised* He will meet you at the altar.

2. Come away from the busyness and *come* unto Him.

3. *Bow* before the Lord in humility and worship.

4. *Kneel* before Him softening your heart and soul.

5. *Call*, expecting the Lord to answer you (no voicemail).

6. We are His. He *initiated* your relationship with Him.

7. *Sabbath*. Worship and rest today from work.

Reflection

Take your first steps:

- Create a playlist of your favorite worship songs.

- Find or step into your "spiritual prayer closet" each day.

- Sit, bow, or kneel declaring you are there to meet Him.

- Begin by welcoming His Presence.

- Sing with one of the songs or sing your own song.

- Sing until your mind stops thinking about other things.

- Stay involved. Stay alert to the still small voice of God.

- The Lord by His Spirit will begin interacting with you.

- Begin praying and meditating on the Names of the Lord.

- He is Jehovah God, the Lord Jesus, Savior and Lord.
- He is El Shaddai, God Almighty, More than Enough.
- He is the Lord Who Provides All of Our Needs.
- He is the Lord Who Heals and Makes Us Whole.
- He is the Lord Who Encourages His People.
- He is the Lord Who Reconciles Us to Himself.
- He is the Lord Who Fills Us with Righteousness.
- He is the Lord Our Peace Who Calms Every Storm.

- Be sensitive to His nearness and His Presence.

- Listen for His promptings to worship and pray.

- Listen for His leading concerning this section's Scriptures.

- Ask the Holy Spirit to illumine the Lord Jesus to you as you pray through the Scriptures.

- The Lord wants to reveal Himself, His Word, and His Way.

- Thank the Lord for meeting with you; praise His Name.

Through the Day

Continue to keep the Lord, His Word, and His Spirit in your thoughts. Throughout the day, *meditate* on the verses of Scripture.

Expect the Holy Spirit to give you a unique perspective that will benefit you as well as those in and around your life. Be a good listener. Listen for a word of encouragement or instruction. Perform a small act of kindness. Stay focused.

> *Lord Jesus, encourage me with these simple suggestions. Please continue to speak to me and lead me onward and upward. Help me to take the things You are teaching me and weave them into my heart and life. As the deer pants for streams of water, my soul pants for You, O Lord, my Redeemer. Amen.*

Response

Notes

SECTION TWO

THE ALTAR'ED PATTERN

Build the altar of the Lord your God with fieldstones
and offer burnt offerings on it to the Lord your God.
—DEUTERONOMY 27:6

1

Noah Built an Altar to the Lord

Then Noah built an altar to the Lord and, taking some of all the clean animals and clean birds, he sacrificed burnt offerings on it (Genesis 8:20).

Noah, son of Lamech, grandson of Methuselah, was the tenth from Adam in Seth's line. He is best known as the man who built an ark and survived a global flood with his family and the earth's animals, but Noah was much more. Genesis 6:8-9 tells us that Noah was a righteous man, blameless among the people of his time, and like his great-grandfather Enoch he walked with God. Noah was not only a righteous man but also preacher of righteousness (see 2 Pet. 2:5). His preaching foretold of the coming judgment of God as well as presented the prospect for salvation. The opportunity revealed in the ark Noah built was rejected by everyone but his own family.

Noah found grace in the eyes of the Lord (see Gen. 6:8), but it was his faith that enabled him to warn others about things not yet seen (the rain and subsequent flood) and to build the ark in holy fear. By faith he condemned the world and became an heir of the righteousness that comes by faith (see Heb. 11:7).

Noah was the first man to build an altar to the Lord (see Gen. 8:20). We have few details as to the specific shape of his altar or the precision of its construction. The historical record cites that Noah's altar was of a rough, spontaneous nature. Like Abraham after him, there is no mention of any materials such as metal, bricks, or cut stone.[1] In 1 Kings 18 Elijah used twelve stones. When Elijah repaired the altar of the Lord, which was in ruins, he used the stones to represent each one of the tribes descended from Jacob.

It is likely Noah's altar consisted of either earth or unhewn stones. The altar probably had no fixed shape because it depended greatly upon the materials that were available. Noah may have used a single large rock or stone. More than likely, it was a loosely erected heap of stones, but the most important idea presented by the altar is found in the Hebrew word *mizbeach. Mizbeach* is from the root *zabach*, which means to slaughter or kill for the purpose of offering sacrifice. An altar is literally a place *where one offers a sacrifice to the Lord.*[2]

Noah offered a sacrifice to thank the Lord for His divine provision and protection. Noah gave earth's most precious commodity—life. One of every clean beast and every clean fowl were offered by Noah as both a sacrifice of praise and an exercise of faith. Noah's offering was ceremonially clean (Hebrew: *tahowr*)[3] and acceptable before the Lord.

Noah then set fire to his offering. First, the blood of beasts and birds were shed, then they were offered by burning them with fire. Wood or dry grass was placed upon the altar as fuel to set the sacrifice on fire, which caused the sacrifice to burn and smoke to rise into the air. Genesis 8:21 tells us, "The Lord smelled the pleasing aroma."

Reflection

It is time to build an altar. Start with thanksgiving. Thanksgiving is best shown by a sacrifice of praise. Sacrifice involves cost. Give the Lord a heartfelt praise of overflowing gratitude. Such offered honestly and openly speaks to your desire for His Presence. The Lord dwells in the praise offerings of His people. Offering the Lord such a sacrifice will enlist you toward the altar of His Presence. I urge you to offer yourself as a living sacrifice, holy and pleasing to God—this is your spiritual or reasonable act of worship (see Rom. 12:1).

Response

NOTES

1. Andrew R. Fausset, *Fausset's Bible Dictionary*, s.v. "Altar," http://www.studylight.org/dictionaries/fbd/view.cgi?n=201.

2. Strong, *Strong's Exhaustive Concordance*, H4196, H2076.

3. Ibid., H2889.

2

ABRAHAM BUILT AN ALTAR THERE

When they reached the place God had told him about, Abraham built an altar there and arranged the wood on it. He bound his son Isaac and laid him on the altar, on top of the wood (Genesis 22:9).

The Lord's relationship with Abraham is one of the Bible's frequent subjects. First, the Lord called Abraham to leave his ancestral home and go to a place he would later receive as his inheritance (the Promised Land). By faith, Abraham obeyed and went, even though he did not know where he was going. By faith, he made his home in the Promised Land like a stranger in a foreign country (see Heb. 11:8-9).

Noah's global flood had failed to resolve the idolatrous apostasy of men. Abraham, like Noah, followed in the pattern of living an altar'ed life. Abraham's trek began with the spiritual concept of separation. God called him to leave his family and be separated to God and His purpose. The Hebrew is *qadhash*.[1] *Qadhash* means to consecrate, sanctify, prepare, dedicate; be hallowed, holy, sanctified, or separate. *Qadhash* can refer to days (like the Sabbath) and to places (like the ground around the burning bush), to objects used for worship (the Tabernacle) or to people (like Abraham).[2]

> *The Lord had said to Abram, "Leave your country, your people and your father's household and go to the land I will show you"* (Genesis 12:1).

Because the Lord is righteous, just, faithful, wise, good, and merciful (see Gen. 18:19,25; 19:19; 20:6; 24:27), the Lord alone is God and is worthy to be obeyed and worshiped. In addition to his obedience to the Lord's holy commands, the Lord expected Abraham to worship Him by offering sacrifices upon the altar. The bringing of sacrificial offerings to the Lord was diligently practiced by Abraham, as indicated by the mention of him building several altars.

> *The Lord appeared to Abram and said, "To your offspring I will give this land." So **he built an altar there** to the Lord, who had appeared to him. From there he went on toward the hills east of Bethel and pitched his tent, with Bethel on the west and Ai on the east. **There he built an altar** to the Lord* (Genesis 12:7-8).

> *So Abram moved his tents and went to live near the great trees of Mamre at Hebron, **where he built an altar to the Lord*** (Genesis 13:18).

The Lord's request for Abraham to sacrifice his son, Isaac, tested his faith. Abraham built the altar on Moriah because Abraham reasoned that God could raise the dead, and figuratively speaking he did receive Isaac back from death (see Heb. 11:19).

The story is an allegory or type that represents our heavenly Father willingly placing His only begotten Son on the Cross; the Son willingly laid down His life so we could be saved!

Reflection

Each time Abraham built an altar he offered a sacrifice of great cost. The most costly was that of his own son, to which the Lord declared:

> *Because you have done this and have not withheld your son, your only son, I will surely bless you and make your descendants as numerous as the stars in the sky and as the sand on the seashore. Your descendants will take possession of the cities of their enemies, and through your offspring all nations on earth will be blessed, because you have obeyed me* (Genesis 22:16-18).

Place the things that are dearest to you on the altar of His Presence. Offer them freely. Ask the Lord to speak to you as He spoke to Abraham. He will meet you there.

Response

NOTES

1. Strong, *Strong's Exhaustive Concordance*, H6942.
2. Orr, *International Standard Bible Encyclopedia*, s.v. "Holiness," http://www.studylight.org/encyclopedias/isb/view.cgi?n=4361.

3

ISAAC CALLED UPON THE NAME OF THE LORD

Isaac built an altar there and called on the name of the Lord. There he pitched his tent, and there his servants dug a well (Genesis 26:25).

Isaac must have had tremendous perspective. First, he realized that his parents were quite a bit older than those of his friends. Then, there was the Lord's glorious intervention and provision. One morning Isaac travelled with Abraham to the summit of Moriah. After submitting to his elderly father and willfully being placed on the altar, Isaac heard the voice of the angel and witnessed firsthand the provision of Jehovah Jireh, "the Lord will provide" (see Gen. 22:14). I have imagined him talking excitedly when he arrived home. What joy his reunion with Sarah provided. The Lord had proved Himself again as the Lord God Almighty. He truly was El Shaddai—the God who is more than enough (see Gen. 17:1)!

Years passed. Isaac was on his way to meet Abimelech at Beersheba. The night before their meeting. the Lord spoke to Isaac saying, "Do not be afraid, for I am with you; I will bless you and will increase the number of your descendants for the sake of my servant Abraham" (Gen. 26:24). After Isaac heard the voice of the Lord that night, he built an altar. He then called on the Name of the Lord. His declaration speaks to Isaac's intention of entering, embracing, and enjoying the Presence of the Lord his God. Paul mentioned the importance of calling on the Name of the Lord in his letter to the Romans.

> *For there is no difference between Jew and Gentile—the same Lord is Lord of all and richly blesses all who call on him, for, "Everyone who calls on the name of the Lord will be saved"* (Romans 10:12-13).

By faith, with love, we call upon the Name of Jesus. In His Name bodies are healed, demons are cast out, victories are won, and enemies are overcome. Calling upon the Name of the Lord is more than simply praying to Him—it is about experiencing His grace, goodness, and glory. For example, the prophet said, "Then you will call upon me and come and pray to me, and I will listen to you" (Jer. 29:12). When we call upon Him, He will forgive us, fill us, and then freely flow from us.

Like Isaac, set up your tent in "that place," i.e. His Presence. Pitch your tent at the place where you build your altar. Build with the purpose of making the Lord your God your place of habitation. Why? Because, "If you make the Most High your dwelling—even the Lord, who is my refuge—then no harm will befall you, no disaster will come near your tent" (Ps. 91:9-10). Jesus also spoke of this level of commitment:

> *I am the vine; you are the branches. If a man remains in me and I in him, he will bear much fruit; apart from me you can do nothing. ... If you remain in me and my words*

remain in you, ask whatever you wish, and it will be given you (John 15:5,7).

Reflection

We are God's people. When we seek to live in the altar of His Presence, we do so from the position of family. We have been chosen and called out with others of like precious faith. We are being fitly framed together in Christ Jesus to become a holy temple in the Lord. And in Him we are being built together to become a dwelling in which God lives by his Spirit (see Eph. 2:20-22). Enter His Presence with thanksgiving. Call upon the Name of the Lord. For His Name is our fortress, our shield, and our strength. Call upon His Name—O Immanuel. Ask Him to show Himself on your behalf as Wonderful Counselor, Mighty God, and Everlasting Father (see Isa. 9:6).

Response

4

ISAAC BUILT AN ALTAR AND HIS MEN DUG A WELL

Isaac built an altar there and called on the name of the Lord. There he pitched his tent, and there his servants dug a well (Genesis 26:25).

Beersheba is one of the oldest places in Israel. The city marked the southern edge of Canaan and the boundary of cultivated land. Water was an important commodity along the edge of the arid high Judean desert. According to the Bible, the city was founded when Abimelech and Abraham entered into covenant after settling their differences over the well that Abraham had previously dug.[1]

Several years later, Isaac and his men returned to the Beersheba area. The Philistines had stopped up most of the wells after Abraham died. Isaac's men reopened the wells but were in need of more water for their flocks. They began digging new wells and soon discovered a well of fresh water. Their discovery created a running dispute with the herdsmen of Gerar who declared the land and water rights belonged to them. Isaac and the herdsmen quarreled over the first two wells, but when Isaac struck water in the third, no one quarreled over it (see Gen. 26:18-23). Verse 22 says that Isaac named the well Rehoboth ("room") and declared, "Now the Lord has given us room and we will flourish in the land."

Isaac is the first one mentioned in Scripture who built an altar *offering sacrifices up to the Lord* while at the same time *digging down* to find fresh water. Isaac's actions are a beautiful picture of the steps we should take as we begin to live an altar'ed life—*offer up, dig down*.

When we dwell in the Lord's Presence with thanksgiving and praise, we should also be digging deep into the Word and ways of the Lord. The room we make for Him, His Word, and His Spirit guarantees that we will have springs of living water to quench our thirst and cause our lives to flourish as a well-watered garden (see Isa. 58:11). How do we draw the water up from the well of salvation?

With joy you will draw water from the wells of salvation. In that day you will say: "Give thanks to the Lord, call on his name; make known among the nations what he has done, and proclaim that his name is exalted. Sing to the Lord, for he has done glorious things; let this be known to all the world. Shout aloud and sing for joy, people of Zion, for great is the Holy One of Israel among you" (Isaiah 12:3-6).

Reflection

The altar of His Presence calls for us to commit to offer up a consistent sacrifice of thanksgiving and praise. The Lord is our home; we are His people. He fills our being with the manifestation of His Presence when we praise Him. His Presence leads us to part company from the things of earth, that we might be attached to the things of heaven. Unspeakable joy (the joy of the Lord) becomes ours when we grasp that we are His holy ground—holy ground from which He speaks His Name, the Name of the Lord. For in His Name is His Presence and fullness of joy forevermore (see Ps. 16:11).

Dig deep into the Word today. Read a passage that brings joy to your heart. Pray His Word. Expect the Spirit to revive and restore. Be made wise with His wisdom. Embrace His joy in your heart and His light in your eyes. Taste Him; His words are more precious than the purest gold; "they are sweeter than honey, than honey from the comb" (Ps. 19:10).

Response

NOTE

1. Orr, *International Standard Bible Encyclopedia,* s.v. "Beersheba," http://www.studylight.org/encyclopedias/isb/view.cgi?n=1272.

5

JACOB BUILT AN ALTAR AT BETHEL

Then come, let us go up to Bethel, where I will build an altar to God, who answered me in the day of my distress and who has been with me wherever I have gone (Genesis 35:3).

In Genesis 28, Jacob arrived at a town that originally was called Luz. Just outside of town he spent the night at "a certain place" (Gen. 28:11). The word for "place" is the Hebrew word *maqowm*, meaning "a high or sacred place, a sanctuary."[1] Early the next morning Jacob set up a pillar of stone and poured oil on the stone in recognition of the dream he had experienced the night before. He dreamed that a ladder reached into heaven with angels of God ascending and descending on it. He heard the Lord speaking to him and declaring that the covenant made with Abraham and Isaac was still in effect.

Jacob woke from his sleep declaring, "Surely the Lord is in this place; and I knew it not" (Gen. 28:16 KJV). Jacob called the place

Bethel or "house of God." Years later Jacob came to the full understanding that the purposes of God needed to have free course in his life and the lives of his family. The only way this would occur would be for Jacob to return to the altar'ed life. It was Jacob's return trip to Bethel that caused his name change from Jacob to Israel to be permanent.

The promises to Isaac and Jacob are an extension of the Lord apprehending Abraham. Abraham's family was *set apart* for the Lord's purposes. Being *set apart* is the biblical concept called holiness (Hebrew: *qadhash*). The person who is holy belongs to the Lord. The person who is *set apart* to the purposes of the Lord is holy. No one is holy in themselves, but we are holy because we belong to Him and His purpose.

A place where He manifests His Presence is holy ground (Bethel). The tabernacle or temple in which the Lord reveals Himself is a holy building, and all its sacrifices, ceremonial materials, and utensils are holy (see Exod. 28:29; 29:33; 30:25; 1 Kings 8:4). The Sabbath is holy, for it is the Sabbath of the Lord (see Exod. 20:8-11).

Holiness, in short, expresses a relationship that consists of separation from common use and, at the same time, dedication to the service of the Lord.[2] When the Lord changed Jacob's name to Israel and declared blessing upon him, He did so from a piece of ground. The ground was no longer common. It was dedicated ground. The ground became separate and distinct. It was special and holy.

The Lord chose to manifest His Presence in and through Jacob's life and lineage. Thus, the lives of Jacob and his twelve sons were no longer common but dedicated to the will and purposes of God. The injunction, *"Ye shall be holy; for I am holy"* (Lev. 11:44; 19:2) plainly implies both a spiritual and an ethical holiness. Like Jacob, we can't begin to bear a resemblance to the Lord in His divine characteristics. But by the power of the Holy Spirit we can be changed and His

Presence can shine His moral qualities of virtue and love through us.

Reflection

The altar'ed life is a life that presses into the Lord and His Spirit. Pressing in leads to living in His Presence. His full life living in us brings change. This change is ongoing and ever growing for His Name's sake. Ask for His overflowing Presence and show forth His light. Remember:

> *God appeared to him again and blessed him. God said to him, "Your name is Jacob, but you will no longer be called Jacob; your name will be Israel." So he named him Israel* (Genesis 35:9-10).

Response

NOTES

1. Strong, *Strong's Exhaustive Concordance*, H4725.
2. Orr, *International Standard Bible Encyclopedia*, s.v. "Holiness," http://www.studylight.org/encyclopedias/isb/view.cgi?n=4361.

5

MOSES BUILT AN ALTAR CALLED JEHOVAH NISSI

Moses built an altar and called it The Lord is My Banner (Exodus 17:15).

More than four hundred years had passed since Jacob built his altar at Bethel. We might think that the practice of building an altar to the Lord would pass away. Moses had been instructed in the art of pleasing the Egyptian gods. But by faith, Moses refused to be known as the son of Pharaoh's daughter. He regarded disgrace for the sake of Christ as of greater value than the treasures of Egypt because he was looking ahead to his reward (see Heb. 11:24-25). Hebrews tells us that Moses valued the reproach of Christ as greater riches than the treasures in Egypt.

> *By faith he forsook Egypt, not fearing the wrath of the king: for he endured, as seeing him who is invisible. Through faith he kept the passover, and the sprinkling of blood, lest*

73

he that destroyed the firstborn should touch them. By faith they passed through the Red sea as by dry land: which the Egyptians assaying to do were drowned (Hebrews 11:27-29 KJV).

The children of Israel journeyed through the wilderness and camped in Rephidim (see Exod. 17). It was there that Moses followed the instructions of the Lord, striking a rock from which flowed enough water to quench the thirst of the people. Soon after, Amalek launched an attack against Israel. Moses' plan was to send Joshua with the fighting men while he stood above them on the hill with the rod of God in his hand. Moses rightly believed that the power of the Lord was in that rod. He knew once the rod was lifted up (as he had done over the Red Sea, see Exodus 14:16), victory would be won.

The next day Moses lifted the rod and Israel prevailed, but when his arms grew tired he let them down resulting in the battle going against Israel. Seeing the state of affairs, Aaron and Hur found a stone for Moses to sit upon and held his hands steady. The Lord gave Joshua the victory, and to honor the Lord Moses built an altar, calling it the name *Jehovah Nissi*, "the Lord is my Banner" (see Exod. 17:14-15).

The Name of the Lord, Jehovah Nissi, reminds us of the victory and deliverance Jesus Christ won for mankind at the Cross. The Christian's banner is the Cross of Jesus Christ. When the Cross of the Lord Jesus Christ is lifted up we remember, "And having disarmed the powers and authorities, he [Christ Jesus] made a public spectacle of them, triumphing over them by the cross" (Col. 2:15).

The Cross of Jesus Christ is now bare. Our Lord is no longer nailed to the tree. The grave where His body was placed is now empty. He who was dead is now alive! He is resurrected and now ascended to the highest heavens! Death lost its sting and the grave has lost its victory! We have been given the victory through our Lord Jesus Christ (see 1 Cor. 15:57).

Reflection

Moses built an altar reminding the people of the victory. The altar'ed life remembers. The altar'ed life recounts the blessings of the Lord as Psalm 103 tells us to.

> *Praise the Lord, O my soul, and forget not all his benefits— who forgives all your sins and heals all your diseases, who redeems your life from the pit and crowns you with love and compassion, who satisfies your desires with good things so that your youth is renewed like the eagle's* (Psalm 103:2-5).

Remember the Cross. Remember the victory our Lord won with appreciation, celebration, adoration, and expectation today.

Response

7

THEN THE ALTAR WILL BE MOST HOLY

For seven days make atonement for the altar and consecrate it. Then the altar will be most holy, and whatever touches it will be holy (Exodus 29:37).

Moses was a man totally committed to his God. Chosen by the Lord, Moses considered it a privilege to oversee the construction of the Tabernacle. His devotion is revealed by his dedication to the Lord and His people. The Lord honored Moses by speaking to him face to face, as a man speaks with his friend (see Exod. 33:11). Moses understood that when a person, thing, building, or nation is fully devoted to the worship of the Lord, they are holy.

Nothing is holy in itself, but any person or instrument becomes holy by its consecration to Him. A place where He manifests His Presence is holy ground (see Exod. 3:5). The tabernacle or temple in which His glory is revealed is a holy building, and all its sacrifices, ceremonial materials, and utensils are also holy (see Exod. 28:29; 29:33; 30:25; 1 Kings 8:4). The Sabbath is holy because it is the Sabbath of the Lord. The altar and all who touched it were holy as well.

Holiness, in short, expresses a relation that consists in separation from common use and, at the same time, in dedication to the service of Lord. When God called Moses to be His servant He did so from a piece of ground. The ground was no longer common. It was dedicated ground. The ground became separate and distinct and special. So it is with us, who by faith in His promise build an altar to offer ourselves as a holy sacrifice to the Lord. Our prayer closet or meeting place with God is a holy place in time or space. Our worship is holy because it is dedicated to Him.

The Lord has chosen to manifest His Presence to, in, and through our lives. Thus, our lives are no longer common but dedicated to the will and purposes of God. We have obeyed God's command, "Ye shall be holy; for I am holy" (Lev. 11:44; 19:2), which plainly means we are separated from the world and set apart to God. In ourselves, we cannot begin to bear a resemblance to the Lord's divine glory. But by the power of God we have been made temples of the Holy Spirit and enabled to shine forth His glory (like Moses, see Exodus 34:29). The grace of God has imparted the qualities of righteousness and love in which true holiness consists. Moses, David, and Isaiah declared the Lord's divine holiness becomes, above all, an ethical reality convicting men of sin and demanding of those who would stand in His Presence clean hands and a pure heart (see Isa. 3; Ps. 24:3-4).

And the Lord has declared this day that you are his people, his treasured possession as he promised, and that you are to keep all his commands. He has declared that he will set you in praise, fame and honor high above all the nations he has made and that you will be a people holy to the Lord your God, as he promised (Deuteronomy 26:18-19).

Reflection

Consider all that God has done for you. With thanksgiving present every thought, attitude, word, and act as a living and holy sacrifice unto God. Remind yourself that you have been delivered from the power, penalty, and presence of sin through the washing of regeneration (see Titus 3:5). He has washed you in the precious blood of the Lamb and made you holy. Like the early church we must offer all that we are and have as our offering to the Lord, symbolizing that God comes first in our lives. God is calling you to a greater level of devotion. Have you rededicated your life to the Lord since you came to the altar of His Presence? If not, do it now.

Response

APPLICATION

There is a distinct pattern found in the Ark and altar of Noah. The pattern was instituted with the construction of his Ark. Noah built the Ark using gopher wood. Gopher wood is not available today. We don't know if it was as straight as pine or as strong as oak. History doesn't tell us if gopher wood had the beauty of maple or the strength of walnut. Whatever its makeup, we know Noah's Ark was not *comely*. *Comeliness* is an old English word describing beauty, splendor, majesty, or glory. Noah's Ark did not possess any of these attributes. People may have been intrigued, but the ark did not inspire. Perhaps because Noah covered the ark inside and out with *pitch* (see Gen. 6:14).

Pitch is described as "any of various dark, tenacious, and viscous substances for caulking and paving, consisting of the residue of the distillation of coal tar or wood tar."[1] In modern terms, *pitch* seals up cracks and holes by covering. The *pitch* Noah used (*kaphar* in Hebrew) means to cover or to make an atonement.[2] The gopher

79

wood and the pitch are biblical types of Calvary's Cross and the Lord Jesus. Neither were attractive to men, for the Cross was an instrument of torture and execution, and the Bible says concerning Christ, "For he [Jesus] shall grow up before him [the Father] as a tender plant, and as a root out of a dry ground: he [Jesus] hath no form nor *comeliness*; and when we shall see him, there is no beauty that we should desire him" (Isa. 53:2 KJV).

Reflection

Noah's pattern—gopher wood covered with pitch or his altar covered by the body of a clean animal or bird. God's pattern—an old rugged cross covered by the body and the blood of the Lamb of God. Each of these fulfilled God's divine purposes and won the salvation of mankind.

Neither the rocks used to build his altar nor the wood used to build his ark were noteworthy. Significance is found in what was offered *on the altar (sacrifice) and on the ark (pitch)*. Noah's ark and the altar point to the atoning work of Christ Jesus, like the Roman cross that in itself saved no one. The blood shed on the Cross of Christ purchased salvation for all. The atonement describes the glorious work Christ Jesus achieved by His death on the Cross and describes His work of making us, who were enemies, now the friends of God.

Are you now willing to build an altar and meet with God? If your answer is yes, what are you willing to offer to God? The act of building speaks to your coming, and your offering tells of the price of your commitment. Worshiping is not merely a spiritual experience, but it is an act by which the Lord is experienced. Our offering up a sacrifice of praise exposes our heart to the One being called upon.

Through the Day

Remind yourself of these words:

You have longed for sweet peace, and for faith to increase,
And have earnestly, fervently prayed;
But you cannot have rest, or be perfectly blest,
Until all on the altar is laid.

Is your all on the altar of sacrifice laid?
Your heart, does the Spirit control?
You can only be blest and have peace and sweet rest,
As you yield Him your body and soul.[3]

Noah offered his most precious gift. Noah offered himself.

Therefore, I urge you, brothers, in view of God's mercy, to offer your bodies as living sacrifices, holy and pleasing to God—this is your spiritual act of worship (Romans 12:1).

Response

_____

_____

_____

_____

_____

_____

_____

_____

_____

_____

_____

_____

Notes

NOTES

1. Dictionary.com, s.v. "Pitch," http://dictionary.reference.com/browse/pitch.

2. Strong, *Strong's Exhaustive Concordance*, H3722.

3. Hymn by Elisha A. Hoffman, 1905.

SECTION THREE

THE ALTAR'ED PLACE

Send forth your light and your truth, let them guide me; let them bring me to your holy mountain, to the place where you dwell. Then will I go to the altar of God, to God, my joy and my delight.
—PSALM 43:3-4

1

JOSHUA BUILT AN ALTAR OF UNCUT STONES

Then Joshua built on Mount Ebal an altar to the Lord, the God of Israel, as Moses the servant of the Lord had commanded the Israelites. He built it according to what is written in the Book of the Law of Moses—an altar of uncut stones, on which no iron tool had been used. On it they offered to the Lord burnt offerings and sacrificed fellowship offerings (Joshua 8:30-31).

The name *Joshua* is a contracted form of the Hebrew name *Jehoshua* or *Jeshua*. Both carry the meaning, "Yahweh is deliverance" or "salvation."[1] The direct English transliteration of the name *Jehoshua* is Jesus (Greek: *Iesous*), but translated as *Iesous* and Joshua in Acts 7:45 and Hebrews 4:8.

First appearing in Scripture as the attendant of Moses, Joshua was commissioned as one of the spies sent by Moses in Numbers 13 (see Exod. 24:13; Num. 13:8,16). The Lord chose Joshua to lead the nation of Israel into the Promised Land of Canaan and encouraged him by telling Joshua that the Lord God would be with Joshua as He had been with Moses (see Josh. 1:7-9).

Mount Ebal is first visited in Genesis 12:6-7 (it is near Shechem). It was there that Abraham rested and built an altar to Jehovah after He appeared to him. At Mount Ebal Jacob camped after returning from Mesopotamia and bought a field from the children of Hamer, father of Shechem; and he built an altar he called El-Elohe-Israel (see Gen. 33:19-20).[2] After conquering Jericho, Joshua turned toward Ai where Israel suffered a great defeat due to the disobedience of Achan. Joshua led Israel in an act of repentance that led to the victorious destruction of Ai's army and king. Joshua then led Israel almost 30 miles to the valley of Shechem, which was guarded by opposing hills or mounts. Upon the first, Mount Gerizim, the blessings of the law were read before the people (see Deut. 27). Then, after the blessings, Joshua and the elders crossed the valley of Shechem and read the curses of the law on Mount Ebal (see Josh. 8:30-35).

After the reading, Joshua erected a great altar of unhewn stones, plastered with lime and inscribed with the law. Joshua led Israel in this act, which symbolized the setting in place of Jehovah's law as Israel's permanent law in their land of inheritance. The sacrifice offered was their pledge of continued obedience, and the Lord would conquer all their foes and establish them in security (see Deut. 27:2-8).

Similar to the biblical types found in Noah and his Ark, the typology of Joshua building an altar on Mount Ebal is powerfully significant. Mount Ebal, the hill of cursing (a type of Mount Calvary), was the place where Joshua (a type of Jesus) built an altar (a type of the Cross) and offered a burnt offering (a type of the shed blood of Christ Jesus). Such was done on Mount Ebal as a picture of Israel meeting the Lord at the altar in Exodus 30:6:

*Put the altar in front of the curtain that is before the ark of the Testimony—before the atonement cover that is over the Testimony—**where I will meet with you.***

Reflection

Atop the cursed place God has promised to meet with mankind in the Person, Jesus Christ. No vain religion or futile reliance on a charm or spell or any amount of new age philosophy can supply mankind an audience with the God of the ages. Golgotha, the cursed place of the skull known for its executions and torturous villainy, is now empty. The God of the ages calls to people of every creed, color, nation, and race to come and meet with Him—at the altar. Go to the Cross, to the altar. He will meet you there.

Response

NOTES

1. Orr, *International Standard Bible Encyclopedia,* s.v. "Joshua," http://www.studylight.org/encyclopedias/isb/view.cgi?n=5110.

2. Fausset, *Fausset's Bible Dictionary,* s.v. "el-Elohe-Israel," http://www.studylight.org/dictionaries/fbd/view.cgi?n=1095.

2

A WITNESS BETWEEN US THAT THE LORD IS GOD

And the Reubenites and the Gadites gave the altar this name: A Witness Between Us that the Lord is God (Joshua 22:34).

Joshua needed the assistance of every one of Israel's twelve tribes to conquer the Promised Land. This included the two and a half tribes whose portion of land was located east of the Jordan River—Reuben, Gad, and half of Manasseh (see Num. 32:19). At the conclusion of Joshua's conquest, the two and a half tribes returned home (see Josh. 1:12-15; 22:4-9). Their preoccupation with their flocks gave them the reputation of being slow to join in the struggle for Israel's national independence. But on their return home, the tribes decided to build an imposing altar (see Josh. 22:10).

The remaining tribes responded with horror and fear. They believed it was the intention of the renegade tribes to use the huge altar to worship foreign gods. They reminded Reuben, Gad, and Manasseh of Achan's sin and the judgment of Yahweh upon them all (see Josh. 22:20). To which the clans responded:

> *The Mighty One, God, the Lord! The Mighty One, God, the Lord! He knows! And let Israel know! If this has been in rebellion or disobedience to the Lord, do not spare us this day. If we have built our own altar to turn away from the Lord and to offer burnt offerings and grain offerings, or to sacrifice fellowship offerings on it, may the Lord himself call us to account* (Joshua 22:22-23).

They continued, "On the contrary, it is to be *a witness between us and you* and the generations that follow, that *we will worship the Lord at his sanctuary*" (Josh. 22:27).

This thinking is the same found in Hebrews 10:25. The altar'ed life calls for us to meet with the Lord at the altar (directly and indirectly). The indirect meeting is between those of us who are of like precious faith. Paul said:

> *The Spirit himself testifies with our spirit that we are God's children. Now if we are children, then we are heirs—heirs of God and co-heirs with Christ, if indeed we share in his sufferings in order that we may also share in his glory* (Romans 8:17).

The altar of His Presence breaks down the religious barriers that have a tendency to creep in among God's people. When we are focused on meeting the Spirit of the Lord at the altar, the things that try to hinder and separate fall helplessly around us. Instead of separating God's people, meeting the Lord at the altar with others fosters His manifested Presence, which acts like sticky mortar setting in place the living stones He is building together to become the house of God.

> *Consequently, you are no longer foreigners and aliens, but fellow citizens with God's people and members of God's*

household, built on the foundation of the apostles and prophets, with Christ Jesus himself as the chief cornerstone. In him the whole building is joined together and rises to become a holy temple in the Lord. And in him you too are being built together to become a dwelling in which God lives by his Spirit (Ephesians 2:19-22).

Reflection

The Lord loves to see His people at the altar together. Such unity is a witness. It is a witness to the Lord's salvation being free to all people. It is a witness that in Christ there is neither Jew nor Greek, male nor female, slave nor free. Seek out others who will build and go with you. Move beyond the attitude of enduring the ways of those who believe differently, worship differently, or pray differently than you. Ask the Lord to help you embrace others and to enjoy the manifestation of the Lord's Spirit in and through their lives. Their altar'ed life will alter your life!

Response

3

GIDEON BUILT AN ALTAR: THE LORD OUR PEACE

So Gideon built an altar to the Lord there and called it The Lord is Peace. To this day it stands in Ophrah of the Abiez-rites (Judges 6:24).

Two hundred years after Joshua's death, Israel was suffering from a lack of leadership and the relentless plundering of the Amalekite and Moabite people. For over a hundred years the Lord had used these marauding nations as His instrument of chastisement for His apostate people. Affliction led Israel to cry out to the Lord in desperate prayer. In response to their cries, the Lord sent a prophet to remind them of the grace they had previously experienced as well as of the current favor they enjoyed, even in the midst of their apostasy (see Judg. 6:8-10).

Suddenly Gideon found himself in the Presence of the Angel of the Lord. The Angel's visitation to Gideon was quite different than that of earlier judges, who had been moved upon by the Spirit of the Lord to their work. The Angel appeared in a human, yet divine and glorious, form. He interrupted Gideon who was in the midst of threshing his own personal harvest. This type of appearance is called a *christophany*. The Angel of the Lord had appeared in a similar fashion to Abraham, Jacob, and Joshua (see Gen. 18; 32; Josh. 5). But it was Gideon's demand for a sign, as well as the Angel's food being consumed by fire at the touch of His staff, that made Gideon realize his commission came directly from the Lord (see Judg. 6:17,21-22). In response Gideon built an altar and called it *the Lord is Peace*.[1]

The call and first commission of Gideon are closely joined. He is at once commanded to destroy the altars of Baal set up by his father at Ophrah, to build an altar to Yahweh at the same place, and thereon to offer one of his father's bullocks as a sacrifice. There is no reason to look on this as a second version of Gideon's call. It is rather the beginning of his passion and is deeply significant of the accuracy of the story in that it follows the line of all revelation to God's prophets and reformers to begin their work at home.[2]

Gideon naming the altar speaks to his own deliverance. Gideon began in fear and finished in faith. His fear was conquered and his faith released as a result of his building the altar. His peace was like the peace that overcame the most wicked and diabolical of fears faced by the Lord's disciples in John 20:19, which says, "On the evening of that first day of the week, when the disciples were together, with the doors locked for fear of the Jews, Jesus came and stood among them and said, 'Peace be with you!'"

Our Lord is "the God of peace" Who generously gives the "peace of God" that transcends all understanding (see Rom. 15:33; Phil. 4:7). The Lord sends His prophets with the blessing of peace (see Acts 15:33), and as the "Lord of peace," He Himself gives peace at all times and in every way (2 Thess. 3:16).

Reflection

Gideon may have suffered from a lack of self-worth or a sense of inferiority. His being a member of a lesser tribe, an unimportant family, and a youngest son may be one of the reasons he was so afraid until he had stood in the Lord's Presence at the altar where he offered a sacrificial offering. His faith and confidence was founded in the ruling peace described in Colossians 3:15: *"Let the peace of Christ rule in your hearts."* Gideon would tell you today, "Don't be afraid. The Lord is with you! He will not leave or forsake you! Come now into His Presence. Openly offer Him a sacrifice of praise with your voice giving thanks, and receive His peace."

Response

NOTE

1. Orr, *International Standard Bible Encyclopedia,* s.v. "Jehovah-Shalom," www.studylight.org/encyclopedias/isb/view.cgi?n=4902.

2 Ibid.

4

MANOAH SAW AN AMAZING THING AT THE ALTAR

Then Manoah took a young goat, together with the grain offering, and sacrificed it on a rock to the Lord. And the Lord did an amazing thing while Manoah and his wife watched: As the flame blazed up from the altar toward heaven, the angel of the Lord ascended in the flame. Seeing this, Manoah and his wife fell with their faces to the ground (Judges 13:19-20).

Manoah was the father of Samson. No children had been born to Manoah and his wife because she could not have children. One day, an angel of the Lord appeared declaring that she would conceive and bear a child (see Judg. 13:3). She was told her child was to be born and raised a Nazirite so that he might save Israel out of the hands of the Philistines (see Judg. 13:5).

A Nazarite was an Israelite who was to be separated unto the Lord. They were to be an example of *holiness*. A Nazarite was to be separated from wine and strong drink as well as moist and dried grapes. He was not to eat the fruit of the vine and was never to cut any hair from upon his head. A Nazarite was not to touch a dead body, including the dead body of even his closest family members (see Num. 6:2-8).

> That Manoah was a devout man seems certain in view of the fact that, upon hearing of the angel's visit, he prayed earnestly for the angel's return in order that he and his wife might be instructed as to the proper care of the child to be born (Judges 13:8). The request was granted and the angel repeated the instructions. Manoah with true hospitality would have the guest remain and partake of food. The angel refused, but commanded a sacrifice unto Yahweh.[1]

Perhaps out of ignorance, Manoah asked the name of the angel because it was their custom to name a child after the prophet, prophetic person, or angel who spoke for the Lord concerning such things. But the angel gave this answer: "Why do you ask my name? It is beyond understanding" (or "is too wonderful to speak"). Manoah's response was to offer a grain and a burnt offering to the Lord. As he did, *an amazing thing happened at the altar.* The angel disappeared as he ascended in the altar's flame. This resulted in Manoah being given a revelation. At that moment, he realized the angel was the Angel of the Lord (see Judg. 13:14-21).

Manoah's experience is not unusual. Spiritual understanding usually follows obedience. When we offer ourselves as an offering upon the altar of obedience, we foster the manifested glory and Presence of the Lord. Why? The Lord desires obedience above sacrifice. In Hebrew the word *shama'* is translated "to hear" and "to obey" in English.[2]

In its simpler Old Testament meaning...it carries with it the ethical significance of hearing with reverence and obedient assent. In the New Testament a different origin is suggestive of "hearing under" or of subordinating one's self to the person or thing heard, hence, "to obey."[3]

Our obedience brings understanding.

Reflection

Obedience is the supreme test of faith in God and reverence for Him. In prophetic utterances, future blessing and prosperity were conditioned upon obedience: "If you are willing and obedient, you will eat the best from the land" (Isa. 1:19). After surveying the glories of the coming Messianic kingdom, the prophet Zechariah assured the people that, "This will happen if you diligently obey the Lord your God" (Zech. 6:15). Blessing, understanding, and the Lord's manifested Presence are fostered when we come to the altar with a heart of obedience. Come to the altar of His Presence, meet Him and obey today!

Response

NOTES

1. Orr, *International Standard Bible Encyclopedia*, s.v. "Manoah," http://www.studylight.org/encyclopedias/isb/view.cgi?n=5729.

2. Strong, *Strong's Exhaustive Concordance*, H8085.

3. Orr, *International Standard Bible Encyclopedia*, s.v. "Obedience; Obey," http://www.studylight.org/encyclopedias/isb/view.cgi?n=6422.

5

DAVID BUILT AN ALTAR TO THE LORD THERE

David built an altar to the Lord there and sacrificed burnt offerings and fellowship offerings. Then the Lord answered prayer in behalf of the land, and the plague on Israel was stopped (2 Samuel 24:25).

King David is one of the most well-known characters in all of history. His victory over Goliath as a teenager has been recounted again and again for almost three millennia. His bountiful success, both on and off the battlefield, as well as his talent as a harpist, poet, singer, spiritual leader, and king has been widely written about in thousands of books and songs. Without a doubt, King David led a successful and exciting life, overcoming giants of every size and shape.

On one hand David has been commended to be a saint, and yet few men have committed worse crimes. The character of David must remain, like that of everyone, a conundrum only solved by

99

the marvelous grace of God. Though sinful from the moment his mother conceived him, David was a man after God's own heart (see Ps. 51:5; 1 Sam. 13:14). While within his right to conduct a census of the Israelite people (see Exod. 30:12-13), it was the pride within David's own heart that seduced him. Pride caused David to betray his own conscience as well as that of Joab, who was his confidant and the captain of his army.

Grief-stricken after he had counted the fighting men, David was given three choices by the Lord. He could choose three years of famine, three months of enemy pursuit, or three days of plague. David chose to put himself and Israel into the hands of the Lord. In fact, David said to the prophet Gad, "I am in deep distress. Let us fall into the hands of the Lord, for his mercy is great; but do not let me fall into the hands of men" (2 Sam. 24:14). Unlike Saul, who laid the blame on the people (see 1 Sam. 15:21), David typified Him who took on Himself the iniquity of us all, David pleaded on earth as the Lord declared from above, "Enough! Withdraw your hand" (2 Sam. 24:16).

> *On that day Gad went to David and said to him, "Go up and build an altar to the Lord on the threshing floor of Araunah the Jebusite"* (2 Samuel 24:25).

So David went up, as commanded, and built an altar. David refused the generosity of Araunah, who had offered to give the threshing floor, wood, and oxen to the king for his offering. David, insisting to pay Araunah for all the materials, said:

> *"No, I insist on paying you for it. I will not sacrifice to the Lord my God burnt offerings that cost me nothing." ... David built an altar to the Lord there and sacrificed burnt offerings and fellowship offerings. Then the Lord answered prayer in behalf of the land, and the plague on Israel was stopped* (2 Samuel 24:24-25).

Reflection

Jerusalem was saved. David bought the site where he had built the altar. Years later the site (Araunah's threshing floor) became the site of the altar in Solomon's temple. Psalm 30 commemorates the dedication and consecration of the altar and temple site with these words:

> *You turned my wailing into dancing; you removed my sackcloth and clothed me with joy, that my heart may sing to you and not be silent. O Lord my God, I will give you thanks forever* (Psalm 30:11-12).

Even when facing our most difficult of circumstances, no matter the situation or sin, the Lord our God is compassionate and full of mercy. If we will call upon Him, He will answer us. Deliverance is the result when we come to the altar of His Presence and choose to live the altar'ed life. Our weeping may endure for a night, but joy, wonderful joy, does come in the morning (see Ps. 30:5).

Response

6

PRESENT OFFERINGS TO THE LORD ON THE ALTAR

David left Zadok the priest and his fellow priests before the tabernacle of the Lord at the high place in Gibeon to present burnt offerings to the Lord on the altar of burnt offering regularly, morning and evening, in accordance with everything written in the Law of the Lord, which he had given Israel (1 Chronicles 16:39-40).

"In the past God spoke to our forefathers through the prophets at many times and in various ways" (Heb. 1:1). Such communication is in stark contrast with the Lord's general and natural revelation in which all men, by virtue of their very nature as men, share (see Rom. 1:20). The Lord's special and supernatural revelation has always been given to people at certain turning points of history.

David's revelation was given at a point in time to teach others how to foster the Lord's manifested Presence. In the Scriptures,

David is a shepherd, warrior, musician, poet, father, and king. He is best known as a *worshiper.* The key to David's success in life appears to be found in David's love for the Lord and revealed in the words, *"I will bless the Lord at all times; His praise shall continually be in my mouth"* (Ps. 34:1 NKJV).

David saw worshiping people as the Lord's house, body, and dwelling place. David's worship team, led by Zadok the priest, led the Lord's people in praising Him morning, noon, and night (see Ps. 84:4). Zadok introduced:

> *The sounds of joy and gladness, the voices of the bride and the bridegroom, and the voices of those who bring thank offerings to the house of the Lord, saying, "Give thanks to the Lord Almighty, for the Lord is good; his love endures forever"* (Jeremiah 33:11).

Wearing song like a garment of praise, Zadok and his priests came to the altar. As they led the people of Zion in worship, the Lord gave them *"a crown of beauty instead of ashes, the oil of gladness instead of mourning, and a garment of praise instead of a spirit of despair"* (Isa. 61:3). Their ministry changed the praise and worship of the Lord Almighty. They used their voices, percussion, and stringed instruments along with horns and trumpets. Clapping their hands, they danced and shouted unto the Lord with voices of victory (see Ps. 47:1; 149:3).

Entering His gates with thanksgiving and His courts with praise, they gave thanks to the Lord and praised His Name (see Ps. 100:4). *"For the Lord is good and his love endures forever; his faithfulness continues through all generations"* (Ps. 100:5). True praise is the expression of gladness and the rejoicing of the heart; it is a music of the soul and spirit which no language can adequately express (see Ps. 4:7; 33:21; 103:1; 106:2; Luke 1:46; 2 Cor. 9:15).

Reflection: The Lord's Plan of Praise and Worship

- *Declare.* "I will declare Your Name to my brothers" (Heb. 2:12).

- *Publish.* "That I may publish with the voice of thanksgiving, and tell of all thy wondrous works" (Ps. 26:7 KJV).

- *Honor.* "Let my mouth be filled with thy praise and with thy honour all the day" (Ps. 71:8 KJV).

- *Glorify.* "I will praise thee, O Lord my God, with all my heart: and I will glorify thy Name for evermore" (Ps. 86:12 KJV).

- *Worship.* "O come, let us worship and bow down: let us kneel before the Lord our maker" (Ps. 95:6 KJV).

Response

7

ELIJAH REPAIRED THE ALTAR THAT WAS IN RUINS

And Elijah said unto all the people, Come near unto me. And all the people came near unto him. And he repaired the altar of the Lord that was broken down (1 Kings 18:30 KJV).

Elijah appeared seemingly out of nowhere. He simply stood before Israel's idolatrous king, Ahab, without references, recommendations, or resume. The grizzled prophet loudly declared his proclamation, *"As the Lord God of Israel lives,"* his position, *"before whom I stand,"* and his prophecy, *"there shall not be dew nor rain these years, except at my word"* (1 Kings 17:1 NKJV). And with that, Elijah turned and disappeared. There is no doubt that Ahab and his wicked queen, Jezebel, replayed the old seer's words over and over again in their minds. While it did seem to them like Elijah had been overly dramatic, there was that thing about the rain.

Rain did not come for three days, three months, or even three years. Ahab tried to find Elijah by sending his best officer out, but he turned up empty. As quickly as Elijah appeared, he disappeared. At the end of the third year, "the word of the Lord came to Elijah: 'Go and present yourself to Ahab, and I will send rain on the land.' So Elijah went to present himself to Ahab" (1 Kings 18:1-2). Only this time, things were going to be different. The man of God had no intention of vanishing into thin air. This time, he had instructions from the Lord to summon the people from all over Israel and meet Him on Mount Carmel. Ahab was commanded to bring the four hundred and fifty prophets of Baal and the four hundred prophets of Asherah who were being fed at Jezebel's table (see 1 Kings 18:19).

After taunting the false prophets for most of the day Elijah repaired the altar of the Lord, which was in ruins. The desert fox repaired it by taking twelve stones, each one representing one of the tribes descended from Jacob. With the stones he built an altar in the Name of the Lord, and he dug a trench around it large enough to hold water. After arranging the wood in order, he cut the bull into pieces and laid it on the wood. Then he had twelve large jars filled with water poured on the offering and on the wood until the water ran down around the altar and even filled the trench (see 1 Kings 18:30-35).

At the time of evening sacrifice, the prophet Elijah stepped forward and prayed. There wasn't much formality. Elijah prayed openly and fervently:

> "O Lord, God of Abraham, Isaac and Israel, let it be known today that you are God in Israel and that I am your servant and have done all these things at your command. Answer me, O Lord, answer me, so these people will know that you, O Lord, are God, and that you are turning their hearts back again." **Then the fire of the Lord fell** and burned up the

sacrifice, the wood, the stones and the soil, and also licked up the water in the trench (1 Kings 18:36-38).

In response, the people fell on their faces, crying, "The Lord, He is God" (1 Kings 18:39). The great work of Elijah's ministry was complete. The prophets of Baal were then put to death, which was followed by torrential rain in accordance to the word of Elijah and in answer to his prayer (see 1 Kings 18:40-46).

Reflection

Elijah gathered the pieces he needed to repair the altar. Today's church is desperate for such restoration and repair. The pieces needed to repair the altar and meeting place are: 1) The Lord's divine and precious promises; 2) a continued commitment to spending time in adoration, supplication, and intercession each day; 3) the offering of ourselves as a living sacrifice unto the Lord.

Response

107

APPLICATION

In this section, we studied some of the geographical places where altars were built and graced with the Lord's manifested Presence to those of precious faith. These hallowed sites are known either because of the divine revelations or angelic appearances that supplemented the building of an altar. Mostly for sacrificing, sometimes only as a memorial, altars were named. Moses named his *Jehovah Nissi*, and Gideon named his *the Lord is Peace*. Others, like the one built by the leaders of Reuben, Gad, and Manasseh, were not for burnt offering, nor sacrifice, but as a witness and testimony (see Josh. 22:26-27).

Altars were made only of earth or unhewn stone on which no iron tool was used and without steps going up to them (see Exod. 20:24-26). With each of them there was neither spectacle nor decoration allowed. The altar was to be plain and simple, for it was the meeting place between God and man and therefore a place of shedding of blood without which there is no remission of sin (see Lev. 17:11; Heb. 9:22). The altar is a place of interaction with the Lord for us only through the offering of an innocent life.

Reflection

From our solar system's blazing hot sun to the tiniest moon in Jupiter's orbit and everything in between, God has places. An altar is a place of purpose that conveys this truth—*the Lord wants to meet with us.* What could be the purpose of human beings having a meeting place with God? For what purpose would God choose the altar as His place to meet with man? Perhaps you have similar questions about the possible alien visitations or odd manifestations found at Stonehenge or Easter Island.

Apparently, the early patriarchs found the real answer. Surviving worldwide flood, generations-destroying famine, and the loss of mankind's righteousness for sin, Noah, Abraham, Moses, David, and Elijah all built altars. Upon these altars these men of faith offered sacrifices to the Lord as an offering of thanksgiving and praise for the Lord's guidance, protection, sustenance, strength, or blessing. Each one found the altar'ed life as promised in Exodus 30:6.

Each altar had one ultimate purpose. That purpose was to create a meeting place with the Lord God Almighty. The Hebrew mind viewed the altar as a place where men and women came to worship. It was the place where the passion for and the movement toward the Lord came together. At an altar, Abel offered his finest lamb, while Noah's provided a sweet aroma that rose to the Lord. Where Abraham's altar saw the salvation of a promised son; Joshua's celebrated the entrance into the Promised Land. Gideon's altar saw deliverance, and Elijah's changed a nation.

Through the Day

Where is the place that you meet with the Lord? Can you sense the sweet stirrings of the Holy Spirit there? Are you tired of living without passion or unfulfilled purpose? Does your heart still thirst for the living water of the Spirit as the deer pants for a cool mountain stream?

If you haven't found a trysting place, do so now. Find an uncommon place, either in space or time, to get together with the Lord and His people. Meet regularly. Wait patiently. Call expectantly. Pray unceasingly. At the altar, the Lord will meet you. Every meeting you have with Him will alter your life toward the divine plan and purpose given to you by the Lord.

Response

Notes

SECTION FOUR

THE ALTAR'ED ORDER

For because you did not do it the first time, the
Lord our God broke out against us, because we
did not consult Him about the proper order.
—1 CHRONICLES 15:13 NKJV

1

KING DAVID AND THE ARK OF THE LORD

He said to them, "You are the heads of the Levitical families; you and your fellow Levites are to consecrate yourselves and bring up the ark of the Lord, the God of Israel, to the place I have prepared for it. It was because you, the Levites, did not bring it up the first time that the Lord our God broke out in anger against us. We did not inquire of him about how to do it in the prescribed way" (1 Chronicles 15:12-13).

When we speak of the scriptural way to build an altar, there was a "proper or prescribed order" to the stones, the wood, and/or the offering. It was either described to or understood by the participants. Moses described the order to Joshua and to the sons of Aaron (see Deut. 27:4; Lev. 1:7-8). Order was understood by Abraham and Elijah (see Gen. 22:9-10; 1 Kings 18:33). The Hebrew word for order is *'arakh*. The word *'arakh* usually means orderly or proper arrangement. It is akin to the idea of arranging cardinal numbers. Jesus spoke of such, "All by itself the soil produces grain—*first* the stalk, *then* the head, *then* the full kernel in the head" (Mark 4:28).

The altar is a biblical type of the place where we come to meet with the Lord. The importance of the altar's *order* is fully realized in its typical use of Isaiah's prophetic picture of the suffering Servant, Christ Jesus (see Isa. 53:1-7). Other examples include the building of Abraham's altar, the arranging of the wood, and the offering of Isaac. Such is a biblical type of Calvary (building the altar), the Cross (the wood), and the Son (Isaac substituted by Yahweh's ram).

An additional example is found when King David decided to bring the Ark of the Covenant to the place that he had prepared for it (see 1 Chron. 15:3). David's place is similar to Abraham's altar. David wanted to bring the Ark to a place in Jerusalem. The Ark is an Old Testament type of the Lord Jesus Christ. It was made of acacia wood overlaid with gold, both inside and out. The Ark's overlay of gold speaks of Christ's complete divinity, while the acacia wood speaks of His complete humanity (see Luke 1:35; 3:22; 4:18).

David's first try resulted in failure. He was more concerned with what he wanted than following the prescribed order. David failed to consult the Levites. Following the example of the Philistines, David attempted to move the Ark on a cart pulled by two oxen. His failure occurred when the oxen stumbled, tipping the cart. The Ark began to slide, causing Uzzah to catch the Ark with his hand, which resulted in the Lord's anger, Uzzah's death, and David's failure (see 2 Sam. 6).

Months later, David realized that he had failed in following God's order. The Ark represented Israel's coming Messiah and was to only be carried by the priests (see Exod. 25:14). This is so today. The Lord Jesus Christ cannot be carried by a wagon or cart. His residence is not a building or church sanctuary. By the Spirit, He dwells in the hearts of His people and can only be carried and manifested in and through them.

Reflection

It is important for us to recognize the steps in the order of God revealed in the example of David and the Ark. Proper order means 1) preparing a place and 2) embracing His Person and the expression of His Presence. The Holy Spirit longs to do more than to remind us of the words in our Bibles. He seeks to make the Person of the Lord Jesus Christ experientially known to and fully expressed through our lives. His full expression can be prevented and/or limited by many things. Examine your heart and see if there is anything hindering your experience or His expression today.

Response

2

PROPER ORDER: BEGIN WITH THANKSGIVING

He who sacrifices thank offerings honors me, and he prepares the way so that I may show him the salvation of God (Psalm 50:23).

King David submitted to the Lord's proper order. After consulting with the priests and Levites, David ordered their consecration so they could bring up the Ark of the Lord. The priests then carried the Ark to Jerusalem while their brothers traveled along with them singing joyful songs accompanied by cymbals, trumpets, shouting, and dancing (see 2 Sam. 6:14-15).

David poured out his heart before the Lord. He led the joyful procession from the house of Obed-Edom with shouts of joy and thanksgiving (see Ps. 42:4). They brought the Ark of the Lord and set it in its place inside the tent that David had pitched for it. Then David and the priests sacrificed burnt offerings and fellowship offerings before the Lord. When he finished giving the offerings, he blessed the people in the Name of the Lord Almighty (see 2 Sam. 6:17-18).

> *He [David] appointed some of the Levites to minister before the Ark of the Lord, to make petition, to give thanks, and to praise the Lord, the God of Israel. ...***Give thanks to the Lord, call on his name; make known among the nations what he has done*** (1 Chronicles 16:4,8).

King David's order is the antithesis of Paul's description of the disordered apostasy in Romans 1:21, which says, "For although they knew God, they neither glorified him as God nor gave thanks to him, but their thinking became futile and their foolish hearts were darkened." Where disorder is marked by unthankful men, order begins with thanksgiving. David said, "Enter his gates with thanksgiving and his courts with praise; give thanks and praise his name" (Ps. 100:4).

Psalm 118 speaks of the gift of salvation. Salvation makes us a gate of righteousness. Because the righteousness of God continues to fill our lives, we should give thanks to the Lord for His great salvation. Let us give thanks because the Lord has heard our cry and answered us. We will not die but live and will proclaim what the Lord has done (see Ps. 118:17).

Thanksgiving is often brushed aside in all the frantic busyness of life, but it is the very attitude of giving thanks that should last all year long. In the Scripture we are commanded to be thankful. *The Lord wants us to step beyond being people who give thanks (something we do) and become thankful people (who we are).* His true worshipers are the habitation or the "dwelling place" of the Most High God. The Lord has promised to fully dwell in a heart full of gratitude and appreciation.

Since we are receiving a kingdom that cannot be shaken, let us be thankful, and so worship God acceptably with reverence and awe, for our "God is a consuming fire" (Hebrews 12:28-29).

Psalm 107:22 says, "Let them sacrifice thank offerings and tell of his works with songs of joy." Sometimes we do not feel thankful or see the circumstances around us as those for which we should be thankful. In these times we must follow the admonishment of Paul to the Thessalonians, "In every thing give thanks: for this is the will of God in Christ Jesus concerning you" (1 Thess. 5:18 KJV).

Reflection

Choose today and every day to be thankful. Sing of the mercies of the Lord forever. Remind yourself today that He is a great and mighty Savior and Friend. He has redeemed you, called you by name, and you are His. Be thankful for your experience in Him; He will meet you there.

Response

_____

_____

_____

_____

_____

_____

_____

3

PROPER ORDER:
ENTER WITH PRAISE

I will praise thee, O Lord, with my whole heart; I will shew forth all thy marvellous works (Psalm 9:1 KJV).

True praise of God, as distinguished from false praise (Isaiah 29:13; Matthew 15:8), is first of all an inward emotion—a gladness and rejoicing of the heart (Psalm 4:7; Psalm 33:21), a music of the soul and spirit (Psalm 103:1; Luke 1:46) which no language can adequately express (Psalm 106:2; 2 Corinthians 9:15). But utterance is natural to strong emotion, and the mouth instinctively strives to express the praises of the heart (Psalm 51:15 and *passim*). Many of the most moving passages in Scripture come from the inspiration of the spirit of praise awakened by the contemplation of the divine majesty or power or wisdom or kindness, but above all by the

118

revelation of redeeming love. Again, the spirit of praise is a social spirit calling for social utterance.[1]

The Scripture uses two main Hebrew words in describing the act of praise. The first word is *yadah*. The name Judah is *Yadah* in Hebrew (see Gen. 29:35). *Yadah* literally means to throw one's hand. To *yadah* the *Name of the Lord* means to declare and salute. When we *yadah*, we throw or send the power, glory, and value of the Lord's Name.[2] When David led the procession into Jerusalem he gave the Lord *yadah*. After arriving David raised the level of praise to the second Hebrew word—*halal*. He appointed Levites to thank and praise (*halal*) the Lord God of Israel before the Ark (see 1 Chron. 16:4). *Halal* means to shine or to flash forth light in praising or boasting. Such boasting is similar to what we see when a city's favorite sports team wins a world championship at the last moment. It literally means to raise the level of praise until one makes a fool of themselves.[3]

We read of Paul and Silas praying and singing hymns to God in a Philippian jail. At midnight their altar of praise resulted in a ferocious earthquake that shook the foundations of the prison. All at once all the prison doors flew open, and everybody's chains came loose (see Acts 16:25-26). Their thanksgiving and praise created a place for the movement of the Holy Spirit that broke their bonds and set them free.

Our praise should clothe us as a garment and be offered up as a holy sacrifice (see Isa. 61:3; Heb. 13:15). The praise of the Lord is ubiquitously represented in the Bible as much as a duty as it is a natural impulse and delight. To fail in this duty is to withhold from God's glory that which belongs to Him (see Ps. 50:23; Rom. 1:20); it is to shut one's eyes to the signs of His Presence as well as to His great power and mighty strength (see Isa. 40:26); and it is to be unthankful for His kindness (see Gen. 24:27).[4]

Reflection

Let us give to God the honor, glory, and gratitude we owe Him by sincerely cultivating the spirit and habit of praise. Give the Lord your best and highest praise continually as you go through this day. The Scriptures tell us that we can stir the soul by fixing our heart upon the Lord, by meditating on His works and ways, by recounting all of His benefits, and above all—for those alive in Christ Jesus—by dwelling upon the glorious and unspeakable gift of His salvation to us who believe.[5]

> *They encircled the throne and the living creatures and the elders. In a loud voice they sang: "Worthy is the Lamb, who was slain, to receive power and wealth and wisdom and strength and honor and glory and praise!" Then I heard every creature in heaven and on earth and under the earth and on the sea, and all that is in them, singing: "To him who sits on the throne and to the Lamb be praise and honor and glory and power, for ever and ever!"* (Revelation 5:11-13)

Response

NOTES

1. Orr, *International Standard Bible Encyclopedia*, s.v. "Praise," www.studylight.org/encyclopedias/isb/view.cgi?n=6990.

2 Strong, *Strong's Exhaustive Concordance*, H3034, H3027.

3 Ibid., H1984.

4. Orr, *International Standard Bible Encyclopedia*, s.v. "Praise."

5. Ibid.

4

REJOICE IN THE LORD ALWAYS

Rejoice in the Lord always. I will say it again: Rejoice!
(Philippians 4:4)

Noah Webster defined the word *rejoice* in his *1828 American Dictionary of the English Language* as a verb that means "to experience joy and gladness in a high degree; to be exhilarated with lively and pleasurable sensations; to exult." I have no doubt this was the proper order David meant to convey in his song the day he brought the Ark into Jerusalem.

> *Glory in his holy name; let the hearts of those who seek the Lord rejoice. ...Let the heavens rejoice, let the earth be glad; let them say among the nations, "The Lord reigns!"* (1 Chronicles 16:10,31)

Where thanksgiving and praise are offered voluntarily, rejoicing generally follows spontaneously. Such was the situation in 2 Samuel

122

6:14-15 when, "David, wearing a linen ephod, danced before the Lord with all his might, while he and the entire house of Israel brought up the ark of the Lord with shouts and the sound of trumpets." His rejoicing exploded out of a heart filled with thanksgiving and praise. David couldn't help himself. *Dancing with all of his might* was his reasonable and sound response given the situation.

So, why did Paul need to exhort the Church to continually rejoice? Could it be because they had forgotten the Lord is a Father to the fatherless, a Defender of widows, a Rock in a weary land, or a Shelter in time of storm? (See Psalm 61:3; 68:4; Isaiah 32:2.) Had they forgotten the Lord is gracious and full of compassion or that His compassions never fail or that they are new every morning and His faithfulness is great? (See Psalm 111:4; Lamentations 3:22-23.) I think not!

To fully understand Paul's appeal we need to address one of the most-used prefixes in the English language. Prefixes are morphemes which begin words, attaching to a word's main part—the "root" or "stem." For instance, in the word *rejoice*, "re" is the prefix, and "joy" (joice) is the root or stem.

One meaning of the prefix re- is "back." For instance, when you are returning home from an outing, you are turning "back" home. When you reduce the amount of money you spend, you lead it "back" to a smaller amount. When light reflects off a surface, it bends "back."[1]

Another primary meaning of the prefix re- is "again." For instance, when you rearrange the furniture in a room, you arrange it "again" into a different configuration. A marathon runner can become rejuvenated or etymologically made young "again" by sleeping and eating after a long race.[2] EMTs respond to medical emergencies for the purpose of reviving a drowned person or giving them life "again." Such is the idea of the word *revival*, which means to renew or awaken men and women to their spiritual concerns "again."

Reflection

Rejoicing flows out of "replaying" the joy of our salvation, given to us by the Holy Spirit. When we "replay" the joy of whose we are and what we have in Christ Jesus, we "rejoice." Our initial act of rejoicing may feel voluntary. But "rejoicing" revives (again) each time we "replay." Spiritual in nature, rejoicing affects our emotions (see 1 Pet. 1:8-9). Like David, we are made to say, "You have granted me eternal blessings and made me glad with the joy of Your Presence" (see Ps. 21:6).

> *But let the righteous be glad; let them rejoice before God: yea, let them exceedingly rejoice* (Psalm 68:3 KJV).

Response

_____

_____

_____

_____

_____

_____

_____

_____

NOTES

1. "Word Root of the Day: Re," Membean, Quick Summary, accessed September 26, 2016, http://membean.com/wrotds/re-back.
2. Ibid.

5

WORSHIPING IN SPIRIT AND IN TRUTH

Yet a time is coming and has now come when the true worshipers will worship the Father in spirit and truth, for they are the kind of worshipers the Father seeks. God is spirit, and his worshipers must worship in spirit and in truth (John 4:23-24).

The foundational concept of worship comes from the Latin word *pretium*, which means "price" or "value," and should be defined as an ascription of value or worth. Worship has been given to unworthy gods, people, and objects and with improper motives, but true spiritual worship consists in a sincere acknowledgment of real conviction toward the *one true God's* worth. Such is seen in the Book of Revelation where the adoration of our Lord and God fills the highest heavens because He is "worthy" to be worshiped.

Whenever the living creatures give glory, honor and thanks to him who sits on the throne and who lives for ever and ever, the twenty-four elders fall down before him who sits on the throne, and worship him who lives for ever and ever.

They lay their crowns before the throne and say: "You are worthy, our Lord and God, to receive glory and honor and power, for you created all things, and by your will they were created and have their being" (Revelation 4:9-11).

Learning to worship "in spirit and truth" is the next step in the proper order of thanksgiving, praise, and rejoicing. True worship includes purity of heart and purity of expression. True expression flows freely out of the awe, admiration, and adoration one has for the Lord. True worship must be expressed not only with words but also with worshipful emotion and action. Individually and corporately, true worshipers have embraced the altar as the place for expressing sacrificial worship. Beginning with the offering of Abel's best lamb, the offering of thanksgiving was an early element of worship. Whatever its origin, worship as developed in the Old Testament was the expression of gratefulness, adulation, adoration, and the uplift of holy joy before the Creator.[1]

Early corporate worship was largely developed with a true freedom and spirit the temple or synagogue greatly lacked; such was composed of:

1. Enthusiastic prayer (Acts 3; Col. 4:2).

2. Worship consisting of psalms, hymns, and spiritual songs (Col. 3:16; Eph. 5:19).

3. The reading of the Scripture (Col. 4:16; 1 Thess. 5:27).

4. Teaching for instruction and edification (1 Cor. 2:7; 6:5).

5. Prophesying for the purpose of members being specially taught by the Holy Spirit (1 Cor. 14:29-31).

6. Following this came fervent ministry that included participation by those who had come with a hymn, a word of instruction, a revelation, a tongue, or an

interpretation. All of these had to be done in order for the strengthening of the church (1 Cor. 14:26).

7. The meeting closed with the "kiss of peace," the benediction (2 Cor. 13:12; 1 Thess. 5:26; 1 Pet. 5:14).

Reflection

Worshiping in spirit and in truth calls for the continued offering of our lives as living sacrifices (see Rom. 12:1). We must come to God with the right motives and without pride, hypocrisy, or double mindedness (see James 4:3; Job 35:12-13; Ps. 138:6; James 1:6). Not anxious about anything, but in everything, by intention and application with thanksgiving, we should put into practice the altar'ed life. We who worship by the Spirit of God, who glory in Christ Jesus, and who put no confidence in the flesh must press on toward the goal for which God has called us (see Phil. 3:3; 3:14; 4:6).

Response

NOTE

1. Orr, *International Standard Bible Encyclopedia*, s.v. "Worship," http://www.studylight.org/encyclopedias/isb/view.cgi?n=9158.

6

WITH ONE HEART AND ONE MOUTH GLORIFY GOD

May the God who gives endurance and encouragement give you a spirit of unity among yourselves as you follow Christ Jesus, so that with one heart and mouth you may glorify the God and Father of our Lord Jesus Christ (Romans 15:5-6).

The spirit of unity is a concept of God functioning in all believers. The same Spirit of Him who raised Christ from the dead now dwells in each of us. And He who raised Christ from the dead gives life to each of us through His Spirit, Who lives in us (see Rom. 8:11). By the Spirit, our heart instinctively knows exactly what to do to bring blessing to the Lord and His Church. The disunity caused by not forgiving others, not being in proper order, and not worshiping in spirit and in truth often results in relational discomfort and pain.

Something profound occurs when we embrace the order found in the spirit of unity. Unity causes the awareness of the supernatural to be dramatically enhanced—we begin to keenly sense the Holy Spirit in new ways and with greater clarity and comprehension. Such perception makes us aware of our oneness with the Lord and each other. This oneness enables us to have a more intimate knowledge of how to glorify God the Father and the Lord Jesus Christ.

Ezra assembled the Israelites as one man in Jerusalem. Together they began to build the altar of the God of Israel to sacrifice on it. With praise and thanksgiving they sang to the Lord: "He is good; his love to Israel endures forever." And all the people gave a great shout of praise to the Lord, because the foundation of the house of the Lord was laid, resulting in the spiritual reformation of Jerusalem (see Ezra 3:1-2:11).

When Solomon dedicated the temple:

> *The trumpeters and singers joined in unison, as with one voice, to give praise and thanks to the Lord. Accompanied by trumpets, cymbals and other instruments, they raised their voices in praise to the Lord and sang: "He is good; his love endures forever." Then the temple of the Lord was filled with a cloud, and the priests could not perform their service because of the cloud, for the glory cloud of the Lord filled the temple of God* (2 Chronicles 5:13-14).

In the fourth chapter of Acts, the Church came together and prayed.

> *After they prayed, the place where they were meeting was shaken. And they were all filled with the Holy Spirit and spoke the word of God boldly. All the believers were one in heart and mind. No one claimed that any of his possessions was his own, but they shared everything they had. With great power the apostles continued to testify to the resurrection of the Lord Jesus, and much grace was upon them all* (Acts 4:31-33).

These examples tell us that it is a good and pleasant thing when brothers and sisters in Christ live together in unity!

> *It is like precious oil poured on the head, running down on the beard, running down on Aaron's beard, down upon the collar of his robes. It is as if the dew of Hermon were falling on Mount Zion.* **For there the Lord bestows his blessing, even life forevermore** (Psalm 133:2-3).

Reflection

Paul instructs us to be humble, gentle, and patient, bearing with one another in love. We are to make every effort to keep the unity of the Spirit through the bond of peace (see Eph. 4:2-3). Pray that the spirit of unity will dwell in you, flowing toward others without losing any of its mighty power so the body of Christ may be built up until we reach unity in the faith and in the knowledge of the Son of God (see Eph. 4:12-13).

Response

7

THE LORD IS BUILDING HIS HOUSE

When your days are over and you rest with your fathers, I will raise up your offspring to succeed you, who will come from your own body, and I will establish his kingdom. He is the one who will build a house for my Name, and I will establish the throne of his kingdom forever (2 Samuel 7:12-13).

There is no doubt the season of prosperity and peace that David enjoyed was due to him bringing the ark into his tabernacle and the attention he gave to praise and worship. (See 2 Samuel 6 and 1 Chronicles 16.) David basically led a "praise party" and offered a huge choir, orchestra and amount of sacrificial offerings to thank and bless his Lord.

Soon after David realized that he was living in a beautiful "house" of stone and that it was inappropriate for the ark (and the

Presence) of God to be in a tent. He felt it was important for him to build the Lord a "house" worthy of His Name. In response to David's plans the Lord sent David a message declaring that the Lord's "house plans" were much larger than David imagined. Yes, there would be a natural "house" built by David's son, Solomon, but more importantly there would be a spiritual "house" established by another "son" in David's lineage, the Lord Jesus Christ.

Generally speaking, David's tabernacle and order of worship is an Old Testament shadow of New Testament truth. What truth? It is the Lord's will to dwell with and in His people (see Ex 25:8, John 14:23) and to be worshipped in spirit and in truth (see John 4:24). This truth found completion in the incarnation of the Word that "became flesh, and dwelt (Greek "tabernacled") among us," (John 1:14).

Another of the truths realized by David is found in his desire to minister to the Lord through thanksgiving, praise and worship. 1 Chronicles 16:4,7-8 says, "He appointed some of the Levites to minister before the ark of the Lord, to make petition, to give thanks, and to praise the Lord, the God of Israel. That day David first committed to Asaph and his associates this psalm of thanks to the Lord: "Give thanks to the Lord, call on his name; make known among the nations what he has done."

The ark, altar and the tabernacle as a whole, is a picture of the Lord's future plans. The place would become a Person. That Person would present the spiritual and natural spheres of heaven's activity. These Old Testament symbols were but a shadow of the eternal substance, an indication of the true ideal (see Hebrews 8:5; 10:1). The house or tabernacle from which Christ ministered was a tabernacle which the Lord pitched, and not man (see Heb. 8:2).[1]

The writer of the book of Hebrews says, "The Lord Jesus Christ is the High Priest of "the greater and more perfect tabernacle" (Hebrews 9:11). The Lord Jesus Christ in His human manifestation, is both God and man, tabernacle and priest, altar and sacrifice. His people, which are His spiritual body, are now the ambassadors of heaven's plans and purpose (see 2 Cor. 5:20). This "house" is being joined together and rises to become a holy temple in the Lord. We are being built together to become a dwelling in which God lives by his Spirit (see Eph. 2:21-22).

Reflection:

Let's embrace the order of David's tabernacle. Let us minister to the Lord individually and corporately. Let us present ourselves to the Lord both morning and evening. Let us incorporate music, voices and hands to make sacred song. Let us give thanks unto the Lord, for His love endures forever. (See 1 Chronicles 16:39-43.)

Response

NOTE

1. ISBE, Tabernacle #8493.

APPLICATION

Even them will I bring to my holy mountain, and make them joyful in my house of prayer: their burnt offerings and their sacrifices shall be accepted upon mine altar; for mine house shall be called an house of prayer for all people (Isaiah 56:7 KJV).

Isaiah's prophecy declares the redemptive and glorious result of the Cross, resurrection, and ascension. It is important to note the order of the prophet's words. First, the Lord promised to bring the peoples of every nation, creed, color, and race to His Holy Mountain. The mountain mentioned was not Ararat (Noah), Moriah (Abraham), Ebal (Joshua), or Zion (David). He was speaking of the place called Mount Calvary where the blood of Jesus Christ paid the price for mankind's salvation (see Luke 23:33). Second, He was speaking of the mountain John was carried to by the Spirit—to a great and high mountain where John was shown that great city, the holy Jerusalem, descending out of heaven from God (see Rev. 21:10).

Reflection

In that heavenly and eternal place Isaiah saw the Lord's passion for our lives. It is hard for us to understand the ministry of His passion. Why? Humans see eternity from time and see eternity as an extension of time. So when we pray, we speak in time and consequently pray about what was, is, or will be. God, on the other hand, sees time from eternity. He created time *within* eternity. The eternal Spirit Who dwells within us speaks from an eternal perspective. When we do not know how to pray what we ought to pray for, the Spirit Himself intercedes for us (see Rom. 8:26). His intercession is filled with His passion for us. He prays we come to a holy place (the mountain of the Lord), worship a holy Person (the Lord Jesus), and become a holy people (the Church).

Isaiah said the people in the house would be filled with joy. The fulfillment of the prophecy is about the church in Acts 13:52, "And the disciples were filled with joy and with the Holy Spirit," and the modern church in 1 Peter 1:8-9, "Though you have not seen him, you love him; and even though you do not see him now, you believe in him and are filled with an inexpressible and glorious joy, for you are receiving the goal of your faith, the salvation of your souls."

Third, our offerings and sacrifices shall be accepted upon the Lord's altar. Isaiah probably thought about the offerings required by the Law. He didn't know the day would come when the sacrifice of the only begotten Son would be accepted for all people, both Jew and Gentile, for the remission of sin (see Heb. 9:12). Or that the Lord's salvation has made us like living stones, and we are being built into a spiritual house to be a holy priesthood, offering spiritual sacrifices acceptable to God through Jesus Christ (see 1 Peter 2:5). And that in Him the whole building (or house) is joined together and rises to become a holy temple in the Lord. And in Him we too are being built together to become a dwelling that God lives in by His Spirit (see Eph. 2:21-22). This describes the fulfillment of His passion.

Through the Day

Our early study led us to the *promise* that if we would build an altar the Lord would meet us there. In this study we have learned that the altar begins as a *place*, then becomes a *Person*, and finishes as a *people*. Proper order tells us that we are all called to the place of prayer (the Cross) to follow the Person of prayer (the Christ) and to become a people of prayer (the Church). By following proper order we foster God's manifested Presence and open our lives to the Holy Spirit's passion to develop His full expression both in and through our lives.

Response

SECTION FIVE

THE ALTAR'ED PERSON

After six days Jesus took with him Peter, James
and John the brother of James, and led them up
a high mountain by themselves. There he was
transfigured before them. His face shone like the
sun, and his clothes became as white as the light.
—MATTHEW 17:1-2

1

JESUS AND THE TEMPLE

Simeon took him in his arms and praised God, saying: "Sovereign Lord, as you have promised, you now dismiss your servant in peace. For my eyes have seen your salvation, which you have prepared in the sight of all people, a light for revelation to the Gentiles and for glory to your people Israel" (Luke 2:28-32).

Fourteen hundred years after the Promise in Exodus 30:6, the Lord came to the meeting in human form and flesh. Simeon experienced firsthand the Word, Who had entered a new mode of existence and lived in a tent (His physical body) among us (see John 1:1-2,14 Wuest). Without reservation the pre-existent Eternal Word *became flesh* (Greek: *sarx egeneto*).[1] The Lord God Almighty literally transformed Himself. He left eternity for time and moved from heaven to earth. He chose to change from being *the Word* to becoming the *only begotten Son of God*. He Who is I AM has become the Son of Man.

This becoming resulted in the altar (a place of meeting) being replaced in the Person (Jesus Christ) who is the meeting place of God and man. John did not say that the Word entered into a man or dwelt in a man or filled a man. The Word became Man. Trying to explain the exact impact of the Greek word *egeneto* in this sentence is beyond the powers of any human expression. The Word simply *became*—pitching His tent among us. God's created tabernacle revealed the Lord Almighty's Shekinah glory here among us in the Person of God's only begotten Son.

The title *Son of God* fully tells that Jesus Christ is of the same substance as the Father God and intimately related to Him as His Seed and Son. Jesus, the Son of God, the Son of Man, is one Person. Although both God and Man, Jesus is not two persons. Neither is He a mixture of both. He is fully God and man. Through His miraculous conception God interrupted the normal transmission of sin that plagues the human race. Righteousness was transmitted by the seed of the heavenly Father and unrighteousness was eliminated without the transmission of Adam's seed. Only a sinless person could stand in our place taking the punishment our sins deserved.

The Holy Spirit moved upon Simeon that day in the temple enabling him to experience God's manifested Presence and see into the realm of the Spirit. His supernatural insight made him *see the light* in Isaiah 49:6, which says, "I will also make you a light for the Gentiles, that you may bring my salvation to the ends of the earth." Simeon saw the Christ child in the temple—but also as the temple. *The place had become the Person.* No longer would mankind need to come to a place to meet God because God had come to meet mankind in the One called Wonderful, Counselor, Mighty God, the Everlasting Father, and the Prince of Peace.

Reflection

We read of thousands of people coming to see and meet Jesus as He ministered in Capernaum, walked the shores of the Sea of Galilee, healed the sick, and raised the dead. Everywhere He went people came. Some came to be touched, healed, or delivered. Everyone who came in faith realized the promise in Exodus 30:6. In meeting Christ Jesus, people met the Lord at His altar. Sadly, many people continue to seek after God in a place, a mosque, a church building, temple, or synagogue. The Lord can only be found in the Way, the Truth and the Life. His Name is the Lord Jesus Christ. Come to Him in Spirit with thanksgiving, praise, and worship. He will meet you there.

Response

NOTE

1. Strong, *Strong's Exhaustive Concordance*, G1096.

2

JESUS AND THE BAPTIST

Beginning with Genesis and flowing to the end of Revelation, water flows through the pages of Scripture. Genesis 1:2 is the first time water is mentioned. This means that before there was anything— light, sun, or moon, earth, plants, living creatures, or anything else—there was water.

> Many of the great acts of God in history have involved water, such as the parting of the sea (Exodus 14:21), the provision of water for the Israelites in the wilderness (Exodus 15:25; Exodus 17:6), and the crossing of the Jordan River (Joshua 3:14-17). Water is mentioned in several of the Psalms as well as being involved in several of Jesus' miracles (Matthew 14:25; Luke 8:24-25; John 2:1-11).[1]

The most scripturally significant use of water is baptism. The English word *baptism* is a transliteration of the Greek word

141

baptisma, which means immersion by dipping.[2] John, sent by God to prepare the people of Israel for the coming Messiah, taught that water baptism was an outward sign of a person's repentance.[3] The Messiah, Jesus Christ, surprised the Baptist one day by coming and asking John to baptize Him. Why would Jesus (who had no reason to repent) want to be baptized? Jesus told John because "it is proper for us to do this to *fulfill all righteousness*" (Matt. 3:15).

When Jesus was baptized He accomplished a spiritually legal act and publically acknowledged that He was the first altar'ed Person. As Jesus came up out of the water He began praying (building an altar). His baptism and prayer signaled His death as Joseph's adopted son and His life as the only begotten Son of God (literally and prophetically). To which the Father in Heaven responded, "This is my Son, whom I love; with him I am well pleased" (Matt. 3:17).

Luke also wrote, *"And as he was praying, heaven was opened and the Holy Spirit descended on him in bodily form like a dove"* (Luke 3:21-22). This tells us that Jesus took the first step to a lasting change for the human race—legally, spiritually, and literally. Legally, because as the Son of God He took on the temptation of all sin and remained sinless. Jesus Christ lived as a Man who knew no sin. Sinless our Lord qualified as the Lamb able to redeem mankind from the plight of sin.

Change also happened spiritually. Spiritually, because through His death the barrier between God and man was removed. The curtain separating the Holy Place from the Most Holy Place in the temple was torn from the top to the bottom at the moment of His death. *When the curtain ripped a way was made for mankind to enter into the Presence of God.* The shed blood of Jesus redeemed mankind legally, but His death spiritually opened up a new and living way (see Heb. 10:20).

Last, change happened literally. Jesus Christ, who gave Himself for us, redeemed us (legally) from all wickedness. He also purified (literally) for Himself a people that are His very own, making them eager to do what is good (see Titus 2:13-14). Now we are literally able to draw near to God with a sincere heart in full assurance of faith, having our hearts sprinkled (spirit) to cleanse us from a guilty conscience (mind) and having our bodies washed with pure water (body) (see Heb. 10:22).

Reflection

The Altar'ed Person, Jesus Christ, began the process of alteration for all human beings at His baptism. When we follow Him in baptism we are publically testifying that we believe in the work of the Lord Jesus Christ. We accept His work in our stead, and by faith in Him our lives are being altar'ed to a new way of life in Jesus' Name.

Response

NOTES

1. Trent C. Butler, Ed., *Holman Bible Dictionary*, s.v. "Water," (Broadman & Holman, 1991), http://www.studylight.org/dictionaries/hbd/view.cgi?n=6427.

2. Strong, *Strong's Exhaustive Concordance*, G908.

3. Fausset, *Fausset's Bible Dictionary*, s.v. "Baptism," http://www.studylight.org/dictionaries/fbd/view.cgi?n=495.

3

JESUS AND THE SOLITARY PLACE

Very early in the morning, while it was still dark, Jesus got up, left the house and went off to a solitary place, where he prayed (Mark 1:35).

The Lord's altar'ed life is frequently cited in the Gospels. His habit was to attend to prayer early, alone, and for about an hour (see Mark 14:37). Mark's Gospel adds the Lord's appreciation for solitary places. The word *solitary* is *eremos* in Greek. This word is used of places that were uncultivated, deserted, uninhabited, lonely, and desolate.[1] The word also speaks to people who are deprived of the aid and protection of others, especially of friends, acquaintances, kindred, or of women neglected by their husbands as a result of being abandoned.[2]

> The desert [and such solitary places] as known to the Israelites was not a waste of sand, as those are apt to imagine who have in mind the pictures of the Sahara.[3]

145

The *eremos* or solitary place is best known in Scripture as the wilderness where the Nation of Israel wandered for forty years before entering the Promised Land. The Holy Spirit led Jesus into such a place to be tempted by the devil (see Luke 4:1). Most of the solitary places found in Sinai and Palestine are land that needs only water to make it fruitful (see Ps. 65:12).

"Jesus knew what it was to spend a whole night in prayer. He knew the blessing of prayer and the power of prayer."[4] He went off to a solitary place, where He prayed (*k'akei prosêucheto*). Mark pictures Jesus as praying through the early hours between 3 and 6 A.M. It was a place (geographically and spiritually) needing water (the Word and the Spirit) to make it fruitful (change people's lives).

The altar Jesus found in a solitary place qualified as a place of reward. Jesus said, "But when you pray, go into your room [closet], close the door and pray to your Father, who is unseen. Then your Father, who sees what is done in secret, will reward you" (Matt. 6:6). In English a *reward* is something given in recognition of a good act. The *Merriam-Webster Dictionary* defines reward as "something that is given in return for good or evil done or received or that is offered or given for some service or attainment; a stimulus administered to an organism following a correct or desired response that increases the probability of occurrence of the response." The Hebrew word for "reward" is *gamal*, which means to deal fully with as with remuneration or compensation.[5]

> *And without faith it is impossible to please God, because anyone who comes to him must believe that he exists and that **he rewards those who earnestly seek him*** (Hebrews 11:6).

Robertson's Word Pictures says that the premise of God being a rewarder is the "moral necessity to have faith (trust). ...The very existence of God is a matter of intelligent faith so that men are left without excuse."[6] He is a rewarder (*misthapodotês*) to them that seek after (*ekzêtousin*: they that seek out God). Wise and intelligent men still seek Him.

Reflection

The solitary place removed all distractions. The darkness hid the sight of a sinful world. He was open and expressive concerning His requests. Because of His prayer, "The desert and the parched land will be glad; the wilderness will rejoice and blossom. Like the crocus, it [the solitary place] will burst into bloom; it will rejoice greatly and shout for joy" (Isa. 35:1-2). His prayer was rewarded by the Spirit's manifested Presence.

Response

NOTES

1. Strong, *Strong's Exhaustive Concordance*, G2048.
2. Ibid.
3. Orr, *International Standard Bible Encyclopedia*, s.v. "Desert," http://www.studylight.org/encyclopedias/isb/view.cgi?n=2646.
4. Robertson, "Commentary on Mark 1:35," *Robertson's Word Pictures of the New Testament*, http://www.biblestudytools.com/commentaries/robertsons-word-pictures/mark/mark-1-35.html.
5. Strong, *Strong's Exhaustive Concordance*, H1580.
6. Robertson, "Commentary on Hebrews 11:6," *Robertson's Word Pictures of the New Testament*, http://www.biblestudytools.com/commentaries/robertsons-word-pictures/hebrews/hebrews-11-6.html.

4

Jesus Went Out to the Mountain to Pray

One of those days Jesus went out to a mountainside to pray, and spent the night praying to God (Luke 6:12).

Though small in magnitude, the topography of Palestine has a wide range that includes a coastal plain, the Judean desert or wilderness, the Jordan Valley, and two mountainous regions. Within the mountainous region of Galilee lie mountains and hills that tend to average about 2,000 feet above sea level. There are no snowy peaks or glaciers. The lack of great forests and rugged peaks, like those of the Rockies, make them more charming than striking. To the biblical writers they were symbols of eternity as well as the Lord's strength, power, and holiness (see Gen. 49:26; Deut. 33:15; Ps. 65:6,25; Hab. 3:6).

In the Old Testament, mountains speak to the faith of men and the faithfulness of their Lord. Psalm 125:1-2 says, "Those who trust in the Lord are like Mount Zion, which cannot be shaken but endures forever. As the mountains surround Jerusalem, so the Lord surrounds his people both now and forevermore." The Lord met several men of faith either at or on nearby mountains. Abraham met the Lord on Mount Moriah. Moses stood face to face with the Lord on Mount Sinai. Elijah prayed and his sacrifice was consumed by fire falling on Mount Carmel.

Jesus needed to make one of His most important decisions. For months He had been leading a group of followers, some of whom He was teaching and discipling (see Matt. 5:1). His ministry was about to enter its next stage. In the first stage, people came to Jesus. In the second stage, Jesus sent apostles to the people, and prior to choosing them He spent the night in prayer (Greek: *ên dianuktereuôn*). This Greek phrase does not mean He stayed "at the place of prayer" but that He "remained in prayer" until morning. It was commonly used by Greek medical writers who described a night vigil lasting an entire night. Jesus spent the night seeking the Father's guidance in choosing which of the disciples should be His apostles.[1]

This example of praying in the altar of His Presence was expounded upon by the Lord in the eleventh chapter of Luke.

> *Then he said to them, "Suppose one of you has a friend, and he goes to him at midnight and says, 'Friend, lend me three loaves of bread, because a friend of mine on a journey has come to me, and I have nothing to set before him.' Then the one inside answers, 'Don't bother me. The door is already locked, and my children are with me in bed. I can't get up and give you anything.' I tell you, though he will not get up and give him the bread because he is his friend, **yet because of the man's boldness [or persistence] he will get up and give him as much as he needs.** So I say to you: Ask and it will be given to you; seek and you will find; knock and the door will be opened to you. For everyone who asks receives;*

he who seeks finds; and to him who knocks, the door will be opened" (Luke 11:5-10).

Reflection

Everyone is called upon from time to time to make important decisions. While a decision can be examined from different viewpoints, scrutinized as to its possible outcomes, or debated for its effectiveness, followers of Christ Jesus should make decisions from an altar'ed perspective. What does the Lord say about it? Is the Holy Spirit leading or guiding us in a direction or giving us a directive? Be bold. Be persistent. Pray and stay in the altar of His Presence until your prayer and perspective are altar'ed and until they are in line with His.

Response

_____

_____

_____

_____

_____

_____

_____

_____

NOTE

1. Robertson, "Commentary on Luke 6:12," *Robertson's Word Pictures of the New Testament,* http://www.biblestudytools.com/commentaries/robertsons-word-pictures/luke/luke-6-12.html.

5

JESUS AND THE MOUNT OF TRANSFIGURATION

After six days Jesus took with him Peter, James and John the brother of James, and led them up a high mountain by themselves. There he was transfigured before them. His face shone like the sun, and his clothes became as white as the light (Matthew 17:1-2).

It was a day of monumental change. Primitive and crude, brazen and golden—for three thousand years men had built their altars with the things of earth. Lambs and doves, bulls and pigeons, the shedding of their blood and the offering of their flesh had long been accepted to atone for a person's sin. Now the altar was about to become a Person offering His own shed blood as atonement for all sin.

Jesus took His inner circle with Him. Like Abraham, Moses, and Elijah before Him, He climbed a mountain. After leading the little group in a time of worship and prayer, "His clothes became dazzling white, whiter than anyone in the world could bleach them" (Mark 9:3). The Son, the radiance of God's glory, revealed Himself. Of which one witness wrote, "We have seen his glory, the glory of the One and Only, who came from the Father, full of grace and truth" (John 1:14).

The personal experience of Peter, James, and John saw Jesus transfigured before them as the Shekinah glory (*doxa*) of God or, literally, as *the Lord of glory* (see James 2:1). John's words insist that, on that mountain and in that human being, he (John) beheld the majestic, royal, and magnificent glory of Almighty God Who was and is the Logos who existed before time as and with God (see John 1:1-3). "John clearly means to say that 'the manifested glory of the Word was as it were the glory of the Eternal Father shared with His only Son.'"[1]

This glorious transfiguration of our Lord Jesus is best illustrated in the altar and the Hebrew name *Zion*. While *Zion* is a name applied to Jerusalem, or to certain parts of it, nothing certain is known of the meaning except that it is derived from the Hebrew root *tsiyuwn,* meaning a signpost, monument, or market in the sense of being conspicuous.[2]

Like the altar, Zion began as a place. Originally inhabited by the Jebusites, Zion came to be known as Jerusalem. Isaiah said, "The Lord of hosts shall reign in mount Zion, and in Jerusalem, and before his ancients gloriously" (Isa. 24:23 KJV). On the Mount of Transfiguration, the place called Zion, like the altar, became a Person in the Lord Jesus Christ.

> *Out of Zion, the perfection of beauty, God hath shined* (Psalm 50:2 KJV).
>
> *When the Lord shall build up Zion, he shall appear in his glory* (Psalm 102:16 KJV).
>
> *For the Lord hath chosen Zion; he hath desired it for his habitation* (Psalm 132:13 KJV).

Thus saith the Lord God, Behold, I lay in Zion for a foundation a stone, a tried stone, a precious corner stone, a sure foundation: **he that believeth shall not make haste** (Isaiah 28:16 KJV).

Reflection

The Person of the Lord Jesus Christ is the meeting place of God and man. The incarnation, Emmanuel, is God with us. When we come to Christ believing on Him to hear our prayer, we *meet with* God. Jesus offered His life once and for all mankind. Our faith in His Person and work presents us as a holy people before our Father and God.

Response

_____

_____

_____

_____

_____

_____

_____

_____

NOTES

1. Benard, qtd. in Robertson, "Commentary on John 1:14," *Robertson's Word Pictures of the New Testament,* http://www. biblestudytools.com/commentaries/robertsons-word-pictures/john/john-1-14.html.
2. Strong, *Strong's Exhaustive Concordance,* H6725.

6

THEY WENT OUT TO THE MOUNT OF OLIVES

When they had sung a hymn, they went out to the Mount of Olives (Matthew 26:30).

On the mountain as Jesus was praying, "Two men, Moses and Elijah, appeared in glorious splendor, talking with Jesus. They spoke about his departure, which he was about to bring to fulfillment at Jerusalem" (Luke 9:31). The word *departure* is the Greek word *exodos*, which means decease, the close of one's career, or final fate.[1]

> The purpose of the Transfiguration was to strengthen the heart of Jesus as he was praying long about his approaching death and to give these chosen three disciples a glimpse of his glory for the hour of darkness coming. No one on earth understood the heart of Jesus and so Moses and Elijah came. The poor disciples utterly failed to grasp the significance of it all.[2]

155

Now months later Jesus is on His way to another mountain. This time the mountain was a large hill just east of Jerusalem called the Mount of Olives. Hundreds of years earlier the prophet Ezekiel saw the glory of Yahweh go up from the midst of the city and stand "upon the mountain which is on the east side of the city" (Ezek. 11:23 KJV).

> In connection with this the Rabbi Janna records the tradition that the Shekinah stood 3½ years upon Olivet, and preached, saying, "Seek ye the Lord while he may be found, call ye upon him while he is near"—a strange story to come from a Jewish source, suggesting some overt reference to Christ.[3]

Earlier that week Jesus went out of the city, "and stayed on the mountain called Olivet" (Luke 21:37 NKJV). And now, on the lower slopes of the mountain in the Garden of Gethsemane, the Lord Jesus would face His agony—the betrayal by one of His disciples and His arrest.[4]

On reaching the Garden, Jesus said to His faithful but worried young men, "Pray that you will not fall into temptation" (Luke 22:40). As He had done hundreds of times before, He withdrew from them. As was His habit, Jesus prayed. He had prayed in the early morning and through the night. He had built altars in the wilderness and on the mountain. Now, He knelt down in the Garden and poured out His soul, "Father, if you are willing, take this cup from me; yet not my will, but yours be done" (Luke 22:42). The Bible says an angel from heaven appeared to Him and strengthened Him. Being in great anguish, He prayed more earnestly, and His sweat was like drops of blood causing Him to be exhausted from the weight of sin as well its crushing result and remedy.

The Lord Jesus Christ was in complete subjection to the will of His Father. The work for which He came to earth began. That work is the atonement. The atonement is a technical term used to describe what Jesus actually achieved. The word *atonement* means "a making at one," and it describes the work of making enemies friends. He is the mediator of salvation. His mediation is that He gave His life as a sacrifice and propitiation and so gained our redemption.

Reflection

Jesus has brought about reconciliation by mediating (being the altar) between God and mankind. His mediation cost Jesus the sacrifice of His life as a sin offering to God. And He is the *propitiation* for the sins of the whole world (see 1 John 2:2 KJV). The word *propitiation* means to be an atoning sacrifice offered to God to appease His wrath.[5] We were the ones who should have faced God's wrath, but Jesus directed it onto Himself. With God's anger spent on Jesus we can now freely and fully turn to Him and live His altar'ed life. Living His altar'ed life alters our life—forever!

Response

NOTES

1. Strong, *Strong's Exhaustive Concordance*, G1841.

2. Robertson, "Commentary on Luke 9:31," *Robertson's Word Pictures of the New Testament*, http://www.biblestudytools.com/commentaries/robertsons-word-pictures/luke/luke-9-31.html.

3. Orr, *International Standard Bible Encyclopedia*, s.v. "Mount of Olives," http://www.studylight.org/encyclopedias/isb/view.cgi?n=6489.

4. Ibid.

5. *Webster's 1828 Dictionary*, s.v. "Propitiation."

7

AT THE PLACE WHERE JESUS WAS CRUCIFIED

At the place where Jesus was crucified, there was a garden, and in the garden a new tomb, in which no one had ever been laid...they laid Jesus there (John 19:41-42).

The prophet had spoken. He had seen into the realm of the Spirit and been given a view of the Lord's Suffering Servant. The sight was no doubt heartbreaking for Isaiah. He had never spoken about crucifixion and especially a man crucified on whom the sin of the world had been laid. I imagine tears rolling down Isaiah's cheeks when he said, "I offered my back to those who beat me, my cheeks to those who pulled out my beard; I did not hide my face from mocking and spitting" (Isaiah 50:6). The Lord's seer then cried

He is despised and rejected of men; a man of sorrows, and acquainted with grief: and we hid as it were our faces from him; he was despised, and we esteemed him not. Surely he

hath borne our griefs, and carried our sorrows: yet we did esteem him stricken, smitten of God, and afflicted. But he was wounded for our transgressions, he was bruised for our iniquities: the chastisement of our peace was upon him; and with his stripes we are healed (Isaiah 53:3-5).

At the top of the place of the skull the Roman soldiers had dug a deep hole in which to slide the base of the cross. The pole that would serve as the stake lay nearby. News had spread up the hill that the one called Jesus of Nazareth had been thoroughly flogged. Pilate's palace guards had then twisted together a crown of thorns and put it on His head. They clothed Him in a purple robe and began mocking Him ardently. In false worship they shouted again and again, "Hail, king of the Jews!" (John 19:3). They struck Him hard in the face.

Ripping away the robe from His body they tore the flesh from His back. Now naked, Jesus attempted to carry the cross beam that would be nailed to the stake. But, with the loss of blood coupled with the weight of mankind's sin, He fell. He fell face first onto the dirty and dusty *Via Dolorosa*. So they picked Jesus up, making Simon carry His cross (see Mark 15:21). On Way of Suffering they led Him as a lamb for the slaughter (see Isa. 53:7-8). His arrival caused the soldiers to focus on their work. Along with two thieves, they crucified our Lord (see Mark 15:27). Those who passed by hurled insults at him, shaking their heads and saying:

"So! You who are going to destroy the temple and build it in three days, come down from the cross and save yourself!" In the same way the chief priests and the teachers of the law mocked him among themselves. "He saved others," they said, "but he can't save himself! Let this Christ, this King of Israel, come down now from the cross, that we may see and believe" (Mark 15:29-32).

Instead of saving Himself, He saved us. On the eternal altar, the Person Jesus Christ died both for us and as us. He took the anger and wrath of God upon Himself and away from us. He paid a debt He did not owe to remedy a debt we could not pay. His payment *redeemed* humanity. He gave Himself for us to redeem us from all wickedness and to purify for Himself a people that are His very own (see Titus 2:14).

Reflection

Near Calvary was a garden. In the first garden, death came through a man (see 1 Cor. 15:21). But in this garden, death would be faced, defeated, and redeemed. In this garden, the human race was liberated from the slavery of sin and death by the payment of the life of the Lord Jesus Christ. The Son of Man came to give His life a ransom for many (see Mark 10:45). Praise God, the ransom was paid once and for all! Hallelujah!

Response

APPLICATION

Now if we died with Christ, we believe that we will also live with him. For we know that since Christ was raised from the dead, he cannot die again; death no longer has mastery over him. The death he died, he died to sin once for all; but the life he lives, he lives to God. In the same way, count yourselves dead to sin but alive to God in Christ Jesus (Romans 6:8-11).

By now you have been spending time both *at the altar* (the place) and *in the altar* (the Person). You have come to Mount Zion, to the heavenly Jerusalem, the Son of the Living God. You have been put into the Person named Christ Jesus. Your coming has brought you into His body, which is the church of the firstborn whose names are written in heaven. You have come to God, the Judge of all men, to

162

the spirits of righteous men made perfect, to Jesus the mediator of a New Covenant (see Heb. 12:22-24).

His Presence has been filling the place where you meet Him. For His promise is sure: "You will seek me and find me when you seek me with all your heart" (Jer. 29:13). As you acknowledge the Lord, learn to recognize His Presence, you must press on to know Him in the power of His resurrection and the fellowship of His sufferings (see Phil. 3:10). "As surely as the sun rises, he will appear; he will come to us like the winter rains, like the spring rains that water the earth" (Hos. 6:3).

Reflection

Embrace His promise, His place, and His Person. A love for thanksgiving, praise, and worship should be emerging in your heart. Being in His Presence should now become as natural to your heart and soul as breathing is to your body.

Freely embrace your new-found awareness and notions in the Spirit. Nourish your inner being with inspiration. Let nothing hinder your expression. Enjoy the Presence with which God has filled you.

Take Your Next Steps

- Expand your playlist of spiritual songs.

- Welcome His Presence by praising Him for His promise.

- Worship with your heart. Don't think about your words.

- The Holy Spirit has been filling you. Keep going until you overflow.

- Love on the Lord. Lift your voice. Lift your heart.

- Fill your car, your house, your work area with Him.

- Pray through each week's *reflection* section.

- Ask the Holy Spirit to illumine the Lord Jesus to you.

- Remember, the Lord is revealing Himself to you.

- Thank Him for living within you. Glorify His Name.

Through the Day

Steal every moment you can. Give those moments to meditation. Consider what you are learning. Remember to keep leaning. Ask the Holy Spirit to pray through you as much as possible (see Rom. 8:26-27). Pray in the Spirit and pray with the understanding also. Sing in the Spirit and sing with the understanding also (see 1 Cor. 14:15). And pray in the Spirit on all occasions with all kinds of prayers and requests. With this in mind, be alert and always keep on praying for all the saints (see Eph. 6:18). Do not put out the Spirit's fire; do not treat prophecies with contempt (see 1 Thess. 5:19-20).

> *Lord Jesus, encourage me with these simple suggestions. Holy Spirit, continue fostering Your manifested Presence. Cause the things I am learning to become permanent in my heart and soul. Saturate, inebriate, satiate, and satisfy my thirsty soul. In Jesus' Name. Amen.*

Response

_____

_____

_____

Application

_____

_____

_____

_____

_____

_____

Notes

_____

_____

_____

_____

_____

_____

_____

_____

_____

_____

_____

_____

SECTION SIX

THE ALTAR'ED PEOPLE

Once you were not a people, but now you are
the people of God; once you had not received
mercy, but now you have received mercy.
—1 PETER 2:10

1

HE BREATHED UPON THEM

And with that he breathed on them and said, "Receive the Holy Spirit" (John 20:22).

Not since the moment Adam was given life had any person experienced such an altering moment. The first alteration came when God breathed into Adam and the man became a living soul (see Gen. 2:7). This resulted in the human race being given the ability to think, feel, walk, talk, and be in relationship with the Creator. This second alteration flowed from the life giving Spirit of the last Adam. The result was the Creator making men and women the Spirit's dwelling place and people. This life altering moment made possible the idea that men, made of earth's dust, would bear the image of the man of heaven (see 1 Cor. 15:45-49). The Spirit created an altar'ed people. His people became the altar of His Presence.

Many continue to see the Holy Spirit as only the breath or wind of God. But He is more than either and both. He is the third Person of the Trinity and, therefore, God Himself. He has submitted to and has been sent by the Father to "reprove the world of sin, and of righteousness, and of judgment" (John 16:8 KJV). He is the One who draws men to the Father and points them to their Savior, Jesus. He is responsible for our new birth as well as being the resident who lives within us. He led Noah, Abraham, and others to the altar'ed place. The Holy Spirit overshadowed Mary so Jesus could be the altar'ed Person. And now this same Spirit who raised Jesus from the dead is living in us and giving life to us as an altar'ed people.

In the first chapter of Genesis, the Spirit of God hovered over the waters. The Spirit (Hebrew: *ruwach*) by definition *flutters or hovers* like a mother bird over her young.[1] Now the Spirit dwells within us. He desires to hover over or be released upon us for the sake of ministry. Like the dove released by Noah, the Spirit was released from Jesus upon His disciples as He breathed upon them. He also told them to receive the Holy Spirit. Just as the Spirit proceeded from the Father upon Jesus (at His baptism), the Holy Spirit is proceeding from the Lord Jesus and is looking for people to rest upon. Our heavenly Father and the Lord Jesus have a real determination toward the Holy Spirit dwelling within us (for salvation) and resting upon us (for ministry).

When the Holy Spirit is resting upon us His Presence can be sensed similarly to the scent of the anointing oil mentioned in Exodus:

> *Make these into a sacred anointing oil, a fragrant blend, the work of a perfumer. It will be the sacred anointing oil. ...Do not pour it on men's bodies and do not make any oil with the same formula. It is sacred, and you are to consider it sacred* (Exodus 30:25,32).

It is important for us to rearrange our thinking. The Holy Spirit is in us. He also desires to rest or manifest His Presence upon us. The anointing is a Person (not a thing). Christ is more than an

169

individual.[2] The apostle Paul unfolded this Messianic mystery in his Epistle to the Colossians.

> *The mystery that has been kept hidden for ages and generations, but is now disclosed to the saints. To them God has chosen to make known among the Gentiles the glorious riches of this mystery, which is Christ in you, the hope of glory* (Colossians 1:26-27).

Reflection

Ask the Lord to help you to become a resting place for the manifested Presence of the Holy Spirit. He is in you. Ask Him to be manifested upon you. Seek after Him. Do not resist Him. Prayerfully receive all He has for you.

Response

NOTES

1. Strong, *Strong's Exhaustive Concordance*, H7307.
2. Kelley Varner, *Corporate Anointing* (Shippensburg, PA: Destiny Image Publishers, 1998), 5.

2

They Were All Together in One Place

When the day of Pentecost came, they were all together in one place (Acts 2:1).

It had taken ten days. That was how long they had been waiting in the Upper Room of the Temple. Not knowing what to expect, 120 believers had prayed and worshiped for days. They were sure of one thing. Their risen Lord had told them to wait until they were clothed with *power from on high* (see Luke 24:49). They waited, and the power came.

> They received a powerful baptism of the Holy Ghost, a vast increase of divine illumination. This baptism imparted a great diversity of gifts that were used for the accomplishment of their work. It manifestly included the following things: The power of a holy life. The power of a self-sacrificing life. ...The power of a cross-bearing

life. The power of great meekness.... The power of a loving enthusiasm in proclaiming the gospel. The power of teaching. The power of a loving and living faith. The gift of tongues. An increase of power to work miracles. The gift of inspiration, or the revelation of many truths before unrecognized by them. The power of moral courage to proclaim the gospel and do the bidding of Christ, whatever it cost them.[1]

Charles Finney said that he had fully experienced this same Presence and that it made him marvel at His power. He said the power permeated the atmosphere and that everyone in the place was charged with the glorious life of God. For Finney, he experienced people humbling and consecrating themselves completely to the Lord Jesus Christ and His power. This caused many people to be converted and saved.[2]

Mr. Finney's experience was almost 200 years ago. But his experience and observations are still valid. Like a great symphony, the ministry of the Holy Spirit is still dependent upon our submission and willingness to minister with Him. Like the various sections of the individual musicians, everyone within a symphony must be committed to play in complete unity. It becomes very obvious if one of the musicians is not fully committed to the intricate timing and precision needed to play their part. It is only when everyone participates completely that the beauty of the written notes comes to life for everyone to hear.

In the same way we must agree to work together with the Holy Spirit. The word *agree* in Greek is of special interest. The Greek word is *sumphoneo*, from which is translated our word *symphony*, meaning a harmonious blending.[3] As altar'ed people we must enter into a harmonious blending by the Spirit's leading. We must embrace a harmonious blending of God's power with our lives. Jesus taught His disciples to pray that things in earth would be harmony with things that are in heaven (see Matt. 6:9-10). An altar'ed life is committed to be in agreement with the Holy Spirit. An altar'ed people can only satisfied with one result—heaven coming to earth with God's goodness, grace, and glory.

Reflection

I urge you to live a life worthy of the calling you have received. Be completely humble and gentle; be patient, bearing with one another in love. Make every effort to keep the unity of the Spirit through the bond of peace. There is one body and one Spirit, just as you were called to one hope when you were called; one Lord, one faith, one baptism; one God and Father of all, who is over all and through all and in all (Ephesians 4:1-6).

Like Elijah's mantle falling upon Elisha, position yourself in prayer to receive His power from on high. Embrace being one with the Spirit of the Lord.

Response

NOTES

1. Charles Finney, "Chapter 2: What Is It?" in *Power from on High: A Selection of Articles on the Spirit-filled Life* (Fort Washington, PA: Christian Literature Crusade, 1944), http://www.ccel.org/ccel/finney/power.iii.html.

3. Ibid.

4. Strong, *Strong's Exhaustive Concordance*, G4856.

3

THEY DEVOTED THEMSELVES

They devoted themselves to the apostles' teaching and to fellowship, to the breaking of bread and to prayer. Everyone was filled with awe at the many wonders and signs performed by the apostles. All the believers were together and had everything in common (Acts 2:42-44).

The devotion of the embryonic church is the devotional standard by which an altar'ed people is measured. Their level of consecration was such that they refused to allow the smallest thing to interfere with their learning, praying, and living. This level of commitment is illustrated in Paul's first letter to the Corinthians. He said, "I appeal to you, brothers, in the name of our Lord Jesus Christ, that all of you *agree* (KJV: 'speak the same thing') with one another so that there may be no divisions among you and that you may be perfectly united in mind and thought" (1 Cor. 1:10).

The first words used in the King James Version of Acts 2:42 are, "They continued steadfastly." An altar'ed life is a steadfast life. Synonyms for *steadfast* include *unwavering, unfaltering, persistent, committed, dedicated*, and *resolute*. Such devotion caused the Acts believers to break the ceiling caused by doubt, fear, and unbelief. Their kind of devotion created an atmosphere of the kind of thinking that enabled them to break through any limitation they faced.

The repetition of their learning, praying, and living solidified their dedication to a Spirit-filled life in their personal belief system. This repetition caused them to raise the level of their relationship with the Lord Jesus Christ and expanded their expectancy, fostering His manifested Presence. The Holy Spirit's manifested Presence literally transformed them into an altar'ed people. Continual connection to the Spirit transformed them. The English word *transformation* comes from the Greek word also translated as *metamorphosis*. *Metamorphosis* at its root means to be radically transformed from the inside out.[1] The example is how the caterpillar becomes a butterfly. It is amazing how a crawling insect can be transformed into a creature of exquisite beauty. But this is exactly what the Holy Spirit did for them and wants to do for us. He desires that we be transformed into an altar'ed people. He wants to alter our lives until we are conformed to the will of God—until there is a release of His divine nature that alters our heart, our soul, and our way of thinking.

What level of devotion and transformation is acceptable to you? Are you willing to be altar'ed and believe that God will bring about *a restoration of all things spoken of by the prophets* (see Acts 3:21)? *Restoration is the work of the Spirit to bring us personally*, the church corporately, and finally the world universally back to its original condition of purity and forward to the purpose, announced by the prophets and the Lord Jesus, for which it was created. Restoration is more than a return to the church's primitive condition; rather, restoration is about advancing toward the fullness of God's original intention.

Reflection

Becoming an altar'ed people calls for our full devotion. We must fully commit to hearing the voice of the Spirit and obeying the illumination He gives from His Word. To achieve this new level of living, we must rid ourselves of the old ways of thinking and replace them with new thoughts. Once new dominant thoughts take root in the heart, they bring new actions resulting in new manifestations of the Holy Spirit's Presence.

Response

NOTE

1. Strong, *Strong's Exhaustive Concordance*, G3339.

4

THE PLACE WAS SHAKEN AND THEY WERE FILLED

After they prayed, the place where they were meeting was shaken. And they were all filled with the Holy Spirit and spoke the word of God boldly (Acts 4:31).

The early church had fully embraced the concept of being the altar of His Presence. After the healing of the crippled man at the Beautiful Gate the Sanhedrin threatened Peter and John and commanded them not to speak or teach at all in the Name of Jesus. After returning to the gathering of believers everyone raised their voices together in prayer to God (see Acts 4:18,24). Luke's record says the prayer was short and to the point. Upon its conclusion the place was shaken and all of them were filled with the Holy Spirit in a dynamic way.

Being filled with the Holy Spirit creates a conscious union. This means that I no longer see myself as a separate person in a relationship with the Lord Jesus Christ but as one, as a branch in the Vine, as a body member in the Head, and as spirit joined to Spirit.

> The fullness of the Godhead is the totality of the Divine powers and attributes, all the wealth of the being and of the nature of God—eternal, infinite, unchangeable in existence, in knowledge, in wisdom, in power, in holiness, in goodness, in truth, in love. This is the fullness of the nature of God—light, life, love; and this has its permanent, its settled abode in Christ Jesus. All that is His own by right is His by His Father's good pleasure also. It was the Father's good pleasure that in Christ should all the fullness dwell.[1]

I am dependent on Him. He permanently is being expressed in me. And so I live spontaneously on this inner fixed truth—the Word is alive in me. Inwardly confirmed by the Spirit I rely on the Spirit to lead and guide, to console and counsel, to empower and endow. This means that I live my daily outer life in total freedom with the inner permanent subconscious reality that it is He living my life by faith (the hidden truth of Colossians 3:4 and Galatians 2:20).

> Faith is the human side of the Divine activity carried on by the Holy Spirit. Faith is therefore implied in the Spirit's action and is the result of or response to it in its various forms. But faith is primarily and essentially faith in Jesus Christ (the Word). Hence, we find that Christ is represented as doing substantially everything that the Spirit does. Now we are not to see in this any conflicting conceptions as to Christ and the Spirit, but rather Paul's intense feeling of the unity of the work of Christ and the Spirit. The "law" of the Spirit's action is the revelation and glorification of Christ Jesus.[2]

This unity of Christ (the Word) and the Spirit enabled the believers in Acts 4 to speak the Word of God boldly. Paul identified the "law" of the Spirit in Ephesians 6:18-19:

Praying always with all prayer and supplication in the Spirit, and watching thereunto with all perseverance and supplication for all saints; and for me, that utterance may be given unto me, that I may open my mouth boldly (KJV).

Reflection

Being filled with and praying in the Spirit brings illumination and expectation to the Word of God. He reminds us of what we have already learned as well as bringing understanding to what we have heard. The result is boldness. Fear, doubt, and unbelief is conquered because we have been given a Spirit of power, love, and self-discipline (see 2 Tim. 1:7).

Response

NOTES

1. Orr, *International Standard Bible Encyclopedia,* s.v. "Fullness," http://www.studylight.org/encyclopedias/isb/view.cgi?n=3580.

2. Ibid., s.v. "Holy Spirit," http://www.studylight.org/encyclopedias/isb/view.cgi?n=4372.

5

ON THE ROAD TO DAMASCUS

As he neared Damascus on his journey, suddenly a light from heaven flashed around him (Acts 9:3).

The time of his conversion [the apostle Paul's] took place just as the gospel was being opened to the Gentiles by Peter (Acts 10). An apostle, severed from legalism, and determined unbelief by an extraordinary revulsion, was better fitted for carrying forward the work among unbelieving Gentiles, which had been begun by the apostle of the circumcision. He who was the most learned and at the same time humblest of the apostles was the one whose pen was most used in the New Testament Scriptures (Ephesians 3:8; 1 Corinthians 15:9). He "saw" the Lord in actual person, which was a necessary qualification for his apostleship, so as to be witness of the resurrection.[1]

The light that flashed around him, blinding his eyes, was the sign of the spiritual light that broke in upon his soul; and Jesus' words to him "to open their eyes and to turn them from darkness to light" (Acts 26:18) were supernaturally reproduced in the theology of his Epistles.[2]

Led into the city of Damascus, Paul no doubt found himself blind and wondering about his earlier experience. The Lord had prepared for his arrival by speaking to a devout man named Ananias.

The Lord said to Ananias, "Go! This man is my chosen instrument to carry my name before the Gentiles and their kings and before the people of Israel. I will show him how much he must suffer for my name" (Acts 9:15-16).

Upon his arrival, Ananias entered the house and placed his hands on Paul. He said, "Brother Saul, the Lord—Jesus, who appeared to you on the road as you were coming here—has sent me so that you may see again and be filled with the Holy Spirit" (Acts 9:17). *It is evident from Paul's ministry and writings that he was filled with the Holy Spirit at that moment.*

The Holy Spirit increased Paul's consciousness as to his relationship with the heavenly Father. No doubt Paul had viewed Yahweh as the Lord Almighty. His understanding was one where God required strict obedience to the law and anyone who strayed from explicit obedience would pay a dear price. By being filled with the Holy Spirit, Paul accepted the teachings of Jesus that taught the austere God of the Old Testament is a kind and gracious loving Father.

Perhaps it was in Damascus that Paul first understood the point he later made to the Ephesians.

Praise be to the God and Father of our Lord Jesus Christ, who has blessed us in the heavenly realms with every spiritual blessing in Christ. For he chose us in him before the creation of the world to be holy and blameless in his sight. In love He predestined us to be adopted as his sons through Jesus Christ, in accordance with his pleasure and will—to the praise of his glorious grace, which he has freely given us in the One he loves (Ephesians 1:3-6).

The love of his heavenly Father changed everything. No longer was Paul convinced that salvation came by perfect obedience to the law, but the love of the Father had been demonstrated by giving His Son for the sin of the world.

Reflection

The love of the Father sent the Son and the Holy Spirit. Love sent Ananias, resulting in Paul taking the good news to the Gentiles. Love pursued and changed Paul and has done the same for millions since. An altar'ed people is a loving people, filled with the Spirit and love of God.

Response

NOTE

1. Fausset, *Fausset's Bible Dictionary*, s.v. "Paul," http://www.studylight.org/dictionaries/fbd/view.cgi?n=2866.

6

PROPHETS AND TEACHERS IN ANTIOCH

While they were worshiping the Lord and fasting, the Holy Spirit said, "Set apart for me Barnabas and Saul for the work to which I have called them." So after they had fasted and prayed, they placed their hands on them and sent them off. The two of them, sent on their way by the Holy Spirit (Acts 13:2-4).

In the church at Antioch there were prophets and teachers (see Acts 13:1). Prophets and teachers had been in the Lord's ministry for thousands of years. Prophetic revelation was not something merely to be experienced, but such was the act of the Lord and His Spirit being experienced. It is the being exposed to, the being moved upon, and the being overwhelmed by Him who desires to reveal Himself.

Prophetic ministry enables us to encounter the Lord in the tension beyond the mystery. The Old Testament is filled with such tension. From Enoch to Malachi the Lord sought to reveal Himself. In the past God had spoken to Israel's fathers through the prophets many times in various ways. In the last days He spoke by his Son, whom He appointed heir of all things and through whom He made the universe (see Heb. 1:1-2).

Through prophetic ministry the indescribable comes in a Voice, disclosing God as a Person who desires to have an altar'ed people. He is not a mysterious puzzle. He is justice, mercy, and love. He is the Person to whom we are accountable, the Pattern and example, and the Power Who manifests His Presence by pouring out His Spirit. He is not unknown. He is the Father, the God of Abraham, Isaac, and Jacob, and out of the endless ages He comes to us with compassion and guidance.

The prophets and teachers in Antioch were given a vision that included the sending of Paul and Barnabas. Their vision was not one of building buildings, nor was it a promise that Paul and Barnabas would have thousands of converts. Nowhere in Paul's writings does he number the people of any churches he established. In fact, outside of the churches he established, most of the Roman Empire knew very little of his ministry or writings.

His was a ministry that operated on scant resources. Much of his last years were spent imprisoned inside cold stone walls. He continued to labor with his own hands and yet he and his ministry were continually met with opposition. Why? He was appointed to be a servant and a witness of what he would see and what the Lord would show him (see Acts 26:16).

The vision that was given to the prophets and teachers was perpetual (see Acts 26:22). The vision included the involvement of others like Silas, Timothy, Titus, and Luke. Paul's part included a conclusion to his ministry and purpose. To those Paul was sent included a time frame, a finish line, and had a reward (see 2 Tim. 4:6-8). Paul finished his portion of the vision. When his portion was complete, the portions assigned to others continued in the process of being fulfilled. As he walked in ministry, his vision became clearer and clearer. Areas he did not fully understand in the beginning became more distinct as natural events confirmed his spiritual understanding.

Reflection

Let us pray that prophetic ministry will be given to those around us. Pray the Holy Spirit will speak through them and that the vision given to them will continue to be fulfilled in our lives, our ministries, and our church. Do not despise prophesying. Embrace God's word for your life today.

Response

7

Paul and the Ephesian Elders

From Miletus, Paul sent to Ephesus for the elders of the church. When they arrived, he said to them: "You know how I lived the whole time I was with you, from the first day I came into the province of Asia. ...I have declared to both Jews and Greeks that they must turn to God in repentance and have faith in our Lord Jesus. And now, compelled by the Spirit, I am going to Jerusalem, not knowing what will happen to me there" (Acts 20:17-18,21-22).

Paul's first visit to Ephesus is recorded in Acts 18:19-21. Some seeds of Christianity may have been sown in the men of Asia present at the outpouring at Pentecost (see Acts 2:9). At his second visit, after his journey to Jerusalem and thence to the eastern regions of Asia Minor, he encountered John's disciples and taught them the baptism of the Holy Spirit and remained at Ephesus three years (see Acts 19:10; 20:31). So this church occupied an unusually large portion of his time and care. His lifestyle of self-denial and unwearied labors are indicated in Acts 20:34. On his last journey he sailed past Ephesus and summoned the Ephesian elders to Miletus (see Acts 20:18-35). Out of his heartfelt feelings and spiritual union with them he delivered to them his farewell charge.

Located on the shore of the Aegean Sea near the northern tip of Asia Minor's western coast, Paul and the Ephesian elders built an altar. Before he left Paul knelt down with all of them and prayed. They all wept as they embraced and kissed him. No doubt because the Ephesians had become an altar'ed people.

Paul had been praying for years:

> *I keep asking that the God of our Lord Jesus Christ, the glorious Father, may give you the Spirit of wisdom and revelation, so that you may know him better. I pray also that the eyes of your heart may be enlightened in order that you may know the hope to which he has called you, the riches of his glorious inheritance in the saints, and his incomparably great power for us who believe* (Ephesians 1:17-19).

Throughout Paul's letter, "the church" is spoken of as one whole in the singular, not the plural. The doctrinal part closes with the sublime doxology (see Eph. 3:14-21). The last half of the Epistle is filled with practical exhortations founded on the counsel of God the Father who is above all, through all, and in all, reared by the "one Lord" Jesus Christ, through the "one Spirit" who gives both gifts and graces to prepare God's people for works of service (see Eph. 4:4-6).

> *so that the body of Christ may be built up until we all reach unity in the faith and in the knowledge of the Son of God and become mature, attaining to the whole measure of the fullness of Christ* (Ephesians 4:12-13).

In conclusion, Paul encouraged this best example of an altar'ed people to not be drunk with wine, which leads to debauchery, but instead to be filled with the Holy Spirit. He sought to stimulate their faith resulting in speaking to one another with psalms, hymns, and spiritual songs. Paul wanted them to sing and make music in their heart to the Lord, "always giving thanks to God the Father for everything, in the Name of our Lord Jesus Christ" (see Eph. 5:18-20).

Reflection

"Pray in the Spirit on all occasions with all kinds of prayers and requests." Be alert and keep on praying. Pray also for your pastors and teachers, that whenever they open their mouths, words may be given them so that they will fearlessly make known the mystery of the Gospel (see Eph. 6:18-20).

Response

APPLICATION

The Lord Jesus Christ is much more than men have ever imagined. There is no one above Him. He has been exalted to the place above all principality and power and might and dominion and every name that is named both in this world and the world to come. His Name is above every name. None are above Him. But with His body it is another story. There is Someone above them. That Someone is the Head of the Church, the Prince of the Lion of Judah, the First and the Last, the Beginning and the End. Bless His Name!

With the founding of His Church, which came in conjunction with the coming of the Holy Spirit, the Holy Spirit organized a community of believers that followed the Lord's principles of discipleship. The pattern for those altar'ed people was, to say the least, radical. He called on His followers to adopt an altar'ed life that served to shape a new people and community. The community was to be one that followed these principles:

- Spirituality—live a life full of the Holy Spirit.

191

- Simplicity—deficiency with regard to this world.

- Purity—separation from the world and to God.

- Humility—overthrow of self in love for one's brother.

- Service—a life filled with adding value to others.

- Community—love expressed through unity.

Reflection

We are the Lord's corporate body, for we are *one* in Him. The Bible calls us sons of God, the body of Christ, and saints of the Living God. We are a chosen generation, a royal priesthood, the dwelling place of God, Abraham's seed, the Lord's brethren, living stones, and many other titles and references. Sometimes we are called by a plural name or title, sometimes by a singular one. For it is a plural body of saints, making up a singular body with Jesus Christ as the Head.

The good news for broken humanity is found in the ministry of the Holy Spirit. The Holy Spirit continues to gather the altar of His Presence. He desires that every person be with the Lord Jesus for eternity. He chose us according to His purpose, blesses us with His Presence, seals us with His power, and fills us with His love.

You, child of God, have received the indwelling blessing of the Spirit of Christ, and it is because God has sent the Spirit of His Son into your heart that you can live by the Spirit and from now on do not have to "gratify the desires of the sinful nature" (Gal. 5:16).

Through the Day

Because Christ lives in you, you now possess sufficient ability to understand any issue, problem, or situation; to make a reasonable decision concerning it; and to know and appreciate the potential consequences of the decision. You are not incompetent. You are:

- Redeemed from the curse of the law (Gal. 3:13).

- More than a conqueror through Him (Rom. 8:37).

- Victorious through the Lord Jesus (1 Cor. 15:57).

- Giving thanks at all times (Phil. 4:4).

- Overcoming the world (1 John 5:5).

As you take your first real steps toward living an altar'ed life you must guard against every attack on your identity. You must remember greater is He that is in you than he that is in the world (see 1 John 4:4).

Response

Notes

SECTION SEVEN

THE ALTAR'ED PURPOSE

Therefore let us leave the elementary
teachings about Christ and go on to maturity...
and God permitting, we will do so.
—HEBREWS 6:1,3

1

The Knowledge of Him Who Called Us

His divine power has given us everything we need for life and godliness through our knowledge of him who called us by his own glory and goodness. Through these he has given us his very great and precious promises, so that through them you may participate in the divine nature and escape the corruption in the world caused by evil desires (2 Peter 1:3-4).

Many believers have given up God's pursuit for the pursuit of happiness, comfort, and consumerism. Peter's letter to the Christ-followers in Asia Minor strikes hard at the heart of such living. Spiritual immaturity, currently an acceptable lifestyle, is causing God's people to be addicted to spiritual Pablum. The modern church, for the most part, has left the *knowledge of Him who called us* for beliefs that are making God's people slow to learn (see Heb. 5:11).

196

The apostle Paul addressed the importance of having the *knowledge of Him* by declaring himself to be an ambassador of Christ (see 2 Cor. 5:20). The proper term for "ambassador" in the Greek is "the emperor's legate."[1] Paul used this dignified term for himself and all ministers of the Gospel. To be effective, the ambassador has to be accepted by both countries (the one that he represents and the one to which he is sent). Paul had to embrace *the knowledge of Him* if he were to act as Christ's legate and act on Christ's behalf and in His stead.[2]

Paul's ambassadorship rested on the experiential knowledge of He who had given Paul the ministry of reconciliation. *Experiential knowledge precedes representation.* A reconciled ambassador is a representative of the Holy Spirit who has the ministry of reconciliation. Paul's words to the Corinthians are clearly saying, "What is true in my life and ministry, as to its source, nature, and authority, is also true of Christ Jesus. He is the One who has sent me, and I am His representative minister—not an exclusive one, but I have given the ministry of reconciliation representing the heavenly Father and Jesus Christ by the Holy Spirit" (see Gal. 2:20).

How can we rightly represent the knowledge of Him? Such representation is the outshining of Jesus Christ 1) by the Holy Spirit and 2) from our lives without any artificial or mechanical means. It is beyond our knowledge of the Bible or any particular theology or philosophy. Representation requires experience with the Holy Spirit. Experience enables understanding. If we are going to be true ambassadors and ministers of Christ and people who are ministering the grace, glory, and goodness of Christ, we must have some deep experiences with Him—very deep experiences. Such experiences cause us to discover something that is of great value to others. Such requires being filled with the Holy Spirit so others can see what it is like for Christ to live in them. Such life is lived by faith in and of the Son of God, who loved us and gave Himself for each of us.

Reflection

The questions are these:

1. Are you growing in the knowledge of Him?

2. Are you emanating the life of Christ?

3. Are you transmitting His goodness, grace, and glory?

4. Is Christ coming through?

5. Are people sensing Christ and not your study, not your library, not your commentaries, not your versions, not your translations, but Christ being truly represented by you in the power of the Holy Spirit?

Enlarge the place of your tent, stretch your tent curtains wide, do not hold back; lengthen your cords, strengthen your stakes (Isaiah 54:2).

Response

NOTES

1. Adolf Deissmann, *Light from the Ancient East* (New York: George H. Doran, 1927), 374.

2. Robertson, "Commentary on 2 Corinthians 5:20," *Robertson's Word Pictures of the New Testament*, http://www.biblestudytools.com/commentaries/robertsons-word-pictures/2-corinthians/2-corinthians-5-20.html.

2

REMOVING OBSTACLES TO KNOWING HIM

You hem me in—behind and before; you have laid your hand upon me. Such knowledge is too wonderful for me, too lofty for me to attain (Psalm 139:5-6).

When we are asked if we "know" someone the question could possess a wide range of meaning. That is not so when it comes to knowing the Lord. The Holy Spirit wants you to have intimate and experiential knowledge of the Lord Jesus Christ. Paul said he considered everything a loss in comparison to knowing Christ Jesus his Lord (see Phil. 3:8). He also told the Ephesians that Christ Jesus desires that "we all reach unity in the faith and in the knowledge of the Son of God and become mature, attaining to the whole measure of the fullness of Christ" (Eph. 4:13).

Such experiential knowledge must be contended for. *Contend* is an intransitive verb meaning to strive or to strive against, to struggle in opposition, to use earnest efforts to obtain, or to defend and preserve. Jude urged those who have been called, "I felt I had to write and urge you to contend for the faith that was once for all entrusted to the saints" (Jude 1:3). The goal of contending for experiential knowledge is Holy Spirit directed and empowered ministry.

Some of us have backgrounds that hinder us from fully embracing the things of the Spirit. These backgrounds can have deep roots. There are five basic root systems that can either grieve or quench the Spirit and war against the changes that the Spirit of God wants to bring to our lives. The first one is "a developed theology that says the gifts of the Holy Spirit ceased, or were severely curtailed, with the close of the Apostolic Age."[1]

This theology is in disagreement with many prominent church fathers:

> Justin Martyr, writing in the middle of the second century, testifies "we see among us today men and women who possess the gifts of the Spirit of God." St. Gregory of Nyssa, who lived in the fourth century, also speaks of contemporaries who possess the gifts of the Holy Spirit: "I know the deeds of our fellow men who walk in the Spirit and give evidences of the power of healing...and have great power against the demons."[2]

In the second century, a man by the name of Irenaeus sat under the teaching of Polycarp, who was discipled by the apostle John. Irenaeus was one of the first church fathers to organize the basic doctrines of the Christian faith. The most famous work of Irenaeus is *Against Heresies* in which he wrote: "In like manner we do also hear many brethren in the Church, who possess prophetic gifts, and who through the Spirit speak all kinds of languages, and bring to light for the general benefit the hidden things of men, and declare the mysteries of God."[3] Irenaeus also said, "Others still, heal the sick by laying their hands upon them, and they are made whole. Yea, moreover, as I have said, the dead even have been raised up, and remained among us for many years. And what shall I more say? Is it not possible to name the number of gifts which the Church, [scattered] throughout the whole world, has received from God."[4]

Reflection

I encourage you to decide today to contend for the experiential knowledge of the Holy Spirit. Ask the Holy Spirit to help you hear the voice of the Lord, activate and mobilize the prophetic words spoken to you or over you, and express your own unique spiritual diversity. Search out articles or books by Dennis Bennett, Arthur Wallis, Beth Moore, Bill Johnson, and Kelley Varner.

Response

NOTES

1. Jerry Munk, "Have the Gifts of the Holy Spirit Ceased?" Living Bulwark, November 2008, Cessation Theology, http://www.swordofthespirit.net/bulwark/nov08p1.htm.

2. Ibid., Ongoing Gifts.

3. Irenaeus, "Book V, Chapter 6.1," in *Against Heresies*, http://www.newadvent.org/fathers/0103506.htm.

4. Irenaeus, "Book II, Chapter 32.4," in *Against Heresies*, http://www.newadvent.org/fathers/0103232.htm.

3

FINDING A PLACE AMONG THOSE WHO ARE

I am sending you to them [the Gentiles] to open their eyes and turn them from darkness to light, and from the power of Satan to God, so that they may receive forgiveness of sins and a place among those who are sanctified by faith in me (Acts 26:17-18).

The second obstacle we must overcome is the idea that God is a respecter of persons. Peter said, "God does not show favoritism but accepts men from every nation who fear him and do what is right" (Acts 10:34-35). Up until the Roman emperor Constantine, total commitment was the dominant lifestyle of believers. Persecution welded the community of believers together, and the ministry of the Holy Spirit was seen to be the responsibility of everyone. With the development of the professional clergy came the idea that only special people had the ability to be used in the gifts of the Spirit.

Church became religious instead of relational. There was a shift from people living in God's Presence to them having a position of administrative authority. Even today, the "exception" in most places is the "preacher." The preacher has "more" than everyone else. Demonstration of the Spirit becomes controlled, reduced, and soon dormant.

This is quite different from the experience of Charles Finney. Finney testified:

> The Holy Ghost descended on me in a manner that seemed to go through me, body and soul. I could feel the impression, like a wave of electricity, going through and through me. Indeed it seemed to come in waves and waves of liquid love; for I could not express it in any other way. It seemed like the very breath of God. ...No words can express the wonderful love that was shed abroad in my heart. I wept aloud with joy and love. ...The waves came over me, and over me, one after the other, until I recollect I cried out, "I shall die if these waves continue to pass over me." I said, "Lord, I cannot bear any more;" yet I had no fear of death.[1]

In 1739, John Wesley wrote in his journal:

> At Weaver's-hall a young man was suddenly seized with a violent trembling all over; and in a few minutes, the sorrows of his heart being enlarged, sunk down to the ground. But we ceased not calling upon God, till He raised him up full of joy and peace in the Holy Spirit.[2]

The apostle Peter testified as well in Acts 10:44-45:

> *While Peter was still speaking these words, the Holy Spirit came on all who heard the message. The circumcised believers who had come with Peter were astonished that the gift of the Holy Spirit had been poured out even on the Gentiles.*

Spiritual qualification comes by grace, not works. The Holy Spirit's demonstration in our lives is not about us earning or achieving. His ministry to, in, and through us has to do with Him overcoming the deception of sin and darkness. It is more about removing obstacles to His moving and the personal baggage we carry than our trying to earn His favor or see a demonstration of His power.

Reflection

> *In the last days, God says, I will pour out my Spirit on all people. Your sons and daughters will prophesy, your young men will see visions, your old men will dream dreams. Even on my servants, both men and women, I will pour out my Spirit in those days, and they will prophesy. ...And everyone who calls on the name of the Lord will be saved* (Acts 2:17-18, 21).

Response

NOTES

1. J. Gilchrist Lawson, "Charles G. Finney: A Brief Biography," in *Deeper Experiences of Famous Christians* (Anderson, IN: Warner Press, 1911), http://www.gospeltruth.net/lawsonbio.htm.

2. John Gillies, "John Wesley's Journal," in *Historical Collections of Accounts of Revival* (Edinburgh: Banner of Truth Trust, 1981), 305, http://quintapress.macmate.me/PDF_Books/Historical_Collections_v1.pdf

4

ROOTED, BUILT UP, AND STRENGTHENED

So then, just as you received Christ Jesus as Lord, continue to live in him, rooted and built up in him, strengthened in the faith as you were taught, and overflowing with thankfulness (Colossians 2:6-7).

Paul used a beautiful illustration in his letter to the Colossians. He ties our life in Christ Jesus to a growing tree. The tree (our life in Christ) is to be rooted in the Presence and power of God's Word and Spirit. Like the faithful man in Psalm 1, deep roots draw up the life (water) of the Spirit enabling us to bear fruit in season and cause our life to not wither. Such a foundation causes us to prosper in all things (see Ps. 1:1-3). Paul continued the metaphor with "building up or continually going and growing up" (present tense). To be strengthened or established is the present passive participle of *bebaioô*, which is the old verb "to make firm or stable."[1]

Spiritual growth and stability does not come from a monastic lifestyle. While monasticism tends to be one of the first things people do to respond to the secularization of the church, history tells us that it isn't "getting away" from the world that changes our lives. The Holy Spirit brings His light, life, and love to our lives as we embrace and enjoy our relationship with Him.

Religion would tell us we haven't done enough to have the power or Presence of the Holy Spirit. The truth is we haven't. But Jesus has! Spiritual development isn't about earning favor but learning the ways of Jesus Christ as taught to us by the Holy Spirit. What are His ways? Jesus prayed, fasted, worshiped, and lived a balanced life.

He spent much time with His Father as well as with people. The lie is that works make us an exceptional person or give us an exceptional ministry. It isn't works. It isn't performance but relationship. Spiritual disciplines are not about earning the power of God but developing relationship with the One Who is the Power and the Glory!

It is not up to us to duplicate what God has done before in the Bible or in history. The flesh tries to put pressure on us to "make something happen." Why? Because the people are coming. They have needs. They are sick or afflicted. They are expecting God to do it again. What is our responsibility? Jude says it is to, "build yourselves up in your most holy faith and pray in the Holy Spirit. Keep yourselves in God's love as you wait for the mercy of our Lord Jesus Christ to bring you to eternal life. Be merciful to those who doubt; snatch others from the fire and save them; to others show mercy, mixed with fear—hating even the clothing stained by corrupted flesh" (Jude 1:20-23).

Reflection

We have learned about the obstacles that have kept many people from experiencing the full manifestation of the Holy Spirit. These obstacles include the belief that God no longer moves by His Spirit to heal, deliver, and speak to us through His spiritual gifts. For others they must overcome the belief that they are not good enough, not called or ordained to full-time ministry. Some people are tempted to go to the default that says, "It is probably God, but it might be me," or, "Those things just don't happen to me." For others we must overcome, "I don't pray enough for that to happen," or, "This can't be God. He wouldn't ask me to do that." Oh, yes He would! He wants to use you as His ambassador to reconcile the lost to Himself! Let Him, today!

Response

NOTE

1. Robertson, "Commentary on Colossians 2:7," *Robertson's Word Pictures of the New Testament,* http://www.biblestudytools .com/commentaries/robertsons-word-pictures/colossians/ colossians-2-7.html.

5

POWER, LOVE, AND SELF-DISCIPLINE

For God did not give us a spirit of timidity, but a spirit of power, of love and of self-discipline (2 Timothy 1:7).

I find it somewhat interesting that the apostle Paul would speak of facing the believer's common enemy "timidity." If Paul were anything, he certainly was not timid. Prior to his conversion he executed the assignment of hunting down new Christians and persecuting them for subverting Judaism. After he met the Lord, Paul opposed Peter to his face because Peter was telling the Gentiles they had to follow Jewish customs (see Gal. 2:11-14). Then, he and Barnabas accepted the call by the church in Antioch and traveled throughout Asia Minor and Western Europe (see Acts 13:1-4). He faced persecution, personal attack, and finally prison, seemingly without an ounce of cowardice.

I believe it was Paul's spiritual son, Timothy, who was the one dealing with timidity. Timidity is epidemic in the modern church. While our world has never been freer from religious persecution, there is tremendous pressure to be politically correct and believe that anyone who holds to the righteous principles of the Scripture is bigoted, judgmental, and uncaring. Paul no doubt saw the destruction timidity does to people.

Many people would really like to pursue the altar'ed life but are afraid of the opinions or reactions of others. Fear destroys faith and especially the confidence faith brings. One day, the Lord and His disciples were crossing the Sea of Galilee. Even though the disciples had the Lord with them in the boat, they became paralyzed by the fear of a late afternoon storm. Rising from His nap the Lord asked those with Him, "You of little faith, why are you so afraid?" (Matt. 8:26). He then stood and rebuked the winds and the waves, and it became completely calm.

Several months later, fear gripped the heart of Peter when, after leaving the boat and walking a few steps on the water to Jesus, he "saw the wind." As he began to sink, Peter cried out:

> "Lord save me!" Immediately Jesus reached out his hand and caught him. "You of little faith," he said, "why did you doubt?" (Matthew 14:30-31)

Fear of circumstances, fear of rejection, and the fear of failure hinders a person from living an altar'ed life. To combat the anxiety of having to fill the shoes of Moses, the Lord said to Joshua, "Be strong and courageous. Do not be terrified; do not be discouraged, for the Lord your God will be with you wherever you go" (Josh. 1:9). King David declared in Psalm 27:3, "Though an army besiege me, my heart will not fear; though war break out against me, even then will I be confident." The Holy Spirit inspired these men, enabling them to overcome anxiety, timidity, and every form of apprehension.

Reflection

The Spirit has given us His power as the power found in the Gospel (see Rom. 1:16). He has filled us with the experiential knowledge of Christ's love (agape), which is the fullness of God (see Eph. 3:19). In His love, there is no fear. In fact, perfect love drives out fear, to the point that fear does not exist in real love (see 1 John 4:18). The self-discipline given us by the Spirit enables enthusiasm for the things of God without inordinate passion or overheated imagination. We are to be serious about the Gospel without being sad or depressed. The Spirit wants to mark our lives with confidence, courage, and calmness. Refuse to allow fear to keep you from fulfilling your altar'ed purpose.

Response

5

BEING DILIGENT TO THE END

We want each of you to show this same diligence to the very end, in order to make your hope sure. We do not want you to become lazy, but to imitate those who through faith and patience inherit what has been promised (Hebrews 6:11-12).

The writer of Hebrews had stressed the importance of leaving the elementary teachings about Christ and going on to maturity. These foundational principles include:

1. repenting from dead works
2. faith in God
3. instruction concerning baptisms
4. the laying on of hands
5. the resurrection of the dead
6. eternal judgment (see Heb. 6:1-2)

While it is important for new Christians to learn and know these basic doctrines, it is sad when those who have been saved for years plateau and become stuck in "spiritual grade school."

The act of abandoning is the prerequisite to going on. One cannot climb the mountain until they first leave the parking lot. The exhortation to leave the basic and move toward maturity is similar to the one in Deuteronomy 6:23: "But he brought us out from there to bring us in and give us the land that he promised on oath to our forefathers." Entering the Promised Land required effort. The wilderness had been Israel's home for 40 years. Their advancement required coming out of fear and coming into the faith and patience that would inherit what had been promised.

Centuries later, the writer of Hebrews was not completely satisfied with the spiritual effort of his audience and spoke to the cause of their immaturity. He saw it including a lack of spiritual diligence. The Greek word for diligence is *spoude* (spoo-day). *Spoude* speaks to a person's sincerity, intensity, earnestness, and diligence.[1] To be spiritually diligent means to be serious with industrious intent about fully realizing the life we have been called to live in Christ Jesus by the power and ministry of the Holy Spirit.

Paul and his ministry team exampled such diligence to the Thessalonians. The Gospel brought by them was not simply with words but with power, with the Holy Spirit, and with deep conviction (see 1 Thess. 1:5). The depth of their conviction stimulated the team's spiritual diligence causing them to instruct the Thessalonians on how to live in order to please God and to urge them in the Lord Jesus to do such more and more (see 1 Thess. 4:1).

Spiritual diligence necessitates focus and determined movement with urgency. Such diligence results in a compensation or reward directly relating to the level of the intensity shown in the focus and determined movement (see Heb. 11:6). Jeremiah said:

"In those days, at that time," declares the Lord, "the people of Israel and the people of Judah together will go in tears to seek the Lord their God. They will ask the way to Zion and turn their faces toward it. They will come and bind themselves to the Lord in an everlasting covenant that will not be forgotten" (Jeremiah 50:4-5).

Reflection

I believe that everyone wants to matter. Each of us want to "become." For the altar'ed life to become our way of life we must have an eager, active, and intense determination to live a life that is pleasing to God and a blessing to others. We must seek to be filled with the Holy Spirit's fullness and pray that He will produce in us a deep and abiding love for others. Such is intentional living. It is living a life filled with spiritual intensity, devotion to the leadings of the Spirit, and spiritual diligence.

Response

NOTE

1. Strong, *Strong's Exhaustive Concordance*, G4710.

7

REQUIRED TO BE FOUND FAITHFUL

Now it is required that those who have been given a trust must prove faithful (1 Corinthians 4:2).

Faithfulness is one of the characteristics of God's ethical nature. It denotes the firmness or constancy of God in His relations with men, especially with His people. It is, accordingly, one aspect of God's truth and of His unchangeableness. ...This unchangeableness the Scripture often connects with God's goodness and mercy, and also with His constancy in reference to His covenant promises.[1]

God has proven His constancy in His covenant promises with Abraham, Isaac, and Jacob and in the truth that the Lord Jesus Christ is the same yesterday and today and forever (see Heb. 13:8).

In his letter to the Corinthians, Paul wrote that he and all ministers (*diakonous*) of the New Covenant are required to execute the commands of the Lord Jesus (see 1 Cor. 3:5).[2] They are called to be stewards of the mysteries of God. The steward or house manager was a slave (*doulos*) under his lord (*kurios*) but an overseer (*epitropos*) over the rest (see Matt. 20:8).[3]

As stewards we are called to be ministers in the Lord's ministry. "The ministry is more than a mere profession or trade. It is a calling from God for stewardship."[4] Stewardship requires faithfulness, which is one of the features of God's ethical nature and the essential requirement for all ministers. In other words, we are required to be faithful like bank clerks in their handling of a customer's money or in other positions like public office. Paul told Timothy, "I thank Christ Jesus our Lord, who hath enabled me, for that he counted me faithful, putting me into the ministry" (1 Tim. 1:12 KJV).

Paul held himself to the standard of being faithful. He also surrounded himself with faithful people. In his letters Paul lists Timothy, Epaphras, Onesimus, and Tychicus as those he considered to be faithful ministers to the Lord Jesus (see 1 Cor. 4:17; Col. 1:7; 4:9; Eph. 6:21). The apostle expressed to the Ephesians the importance of being faithful in the work to which each of us are called.

> *For we are God's workmanship, created in Christ Jesus to do good works, which God prepared in advance for us to do* (Ephesians 2:10).

> *From him the whole body, joined and held together by every supporting ligament, grows and builds itself up in love, as each part does its work* (Ephesians 4:16).

Finally, Jesus told a parable in Matthew 25. The parable is about three men who were given differing levels of talents and how they responded to their particular responsibility. The meaning of the parable affirms the Lord has given every person a varied assortment of skills, capacities, gifts, and abilities. The Lord has the expectation that we steward those talents as faithful servants. The point of the parable is that we are to use whatever we have been given for God's purposes and glory.[5] The rewards and consequences tell us that we are to be faithful concerning the investment of our lives in the Master's service and not waste them.

Reflection

Embracing our altar'ed purpose, living an altar'ed life, and living among an altar'ed people calls for us to be people who are committed to being faithful in our living, giving, praying, and worshiping. Faithfulness is rewarded with opportunity. Those who are faithful in small things are given larger things to be faithful with.

Response

_____

_____

_____

_____

_____

_____

_____

_____

_____

NOTES

1. Orr, *International Standard Bible Encyclopedia*, s.v. "Faithful; Faithfulness," http://www.studylight.org/encyclopedias/isb/view .cgi?n=3335.
2. Strong, *Strong's Exhaustive Concordance*, G1249.

3. Robertson, "Commentary on 1 Corinthians 4:1," *Robertson's Word Pictures of the New Testament*, http://www.biblestudytools.com/commentaries/robertsons-word-pictures/1-corinthians/1-corinthians-4-1.html.

4. Ibid.

5. William Messenger, ed., "The Parable of the Talents (Matthew 25:14-30)," in *Theology of Work Bible Commentary* (Hendrickson Publishers, 2016), https://www.theologyofwork.org/new-testament/matthew/living-in-the-new-kingdom-matthew-18-25/the-parable-of-the -talents-matthew-2514-30.

APPLICATION

There are many reasons why people do not live in the altar of His Presence. There are those who simply do not believe the promise of an altar'ed life (see Exod. 30:6). Many say that promise was for the nation of Israel or Moses or the Levites but not for them. And as Solomon said, as a man thinks in his heart, so is he (see Prov. 23:7).

Reasons for such doubt or unbelief begin with the theological concept of the Lord changing or limiting Himself in different times or dispensations. Historical records, including the personal diaries of men such as Ignatius, St. Francis of Assisi, Jon Huss, John Wesley, George Whitefield, Charles Finney, and many, many others are either ignored or said to be unreliable. Here is an excerpt from the preface of *John Gillies: Historical Collections of Accounts of Revivals*, by the editor Horatious Bonar:

> Many a wondrous scene has been witnessed from the day of Pentecost downwards to our own day, and what better deserves the attention and the study of the believer than

221

the record of these outpourings of the Spirit? Besides the interest that cleaves to them there is much to be learned from them by the Church. To see how God has been working, and to observe the means and instruments by which He has carried on His work, cannot fail to be profitable and quickening. It makes us sensible of our own short-comings, and it points out the way by which the blessing may be secured.[1]

Reflection

For others, the manifestation of God's Presence points only to a person having God's special calling or the possession of a "spiritual secret" that the Holy Spirit only shares with a selected few. These few are believed to be special due to apostolic succession, supernatural knowledge of the Bible, or an out-of-this-world revelation concerning angels, demons, gifts of the Spirit, or some other marvelous anointing that only "certain people" have. These ignore the words of the apostle Paul who wrote:

> *It was he who gave some to be apostles, some to be prophets, some to be evangelists, and some to be pastors and teachers, **to prepare God's people for works of service,** so that the body of Christ may be built up until we all reach unity in the faith and in the knowledge of the Son of God and become mature, attaining to the whole measure of the fullness of Christ. Then we will no longer be infants, tossed back and forth by the waves, and blown here and there by every wind of teaching and by the cunning and craftiness of men in their deceitful scheming. Instead, speaking the truth in love, **we will in all things grow up into him who is the Head,** that is, Christ. From him the whole body, joined and held together by every supporting ligament, grows and builds itself up in love, **as each part does its work** (Ephesians 4:11-16).*

Through the Day

You have been invited to participate in the Lord's goodness, grace, and glory. But, like most people, the layers of doubt, fear, and unbelief have trapped the Shekinah glory of God inside. Will you allow the Spirit to strip away all of the layers that are not Him? Instead of worshiping out of guilt or fear, instead of praying to avert punishment or asking God again to take care of your needs like health, food, and shelter, which are all important things but are secondary to seeking the Kingdom of God and His righteousness— will you ask the Spirit to help you learn His ways? Then, the Spirit can strip away the layers that are not Him. You will experience the ecstasy of being free in Christ Jesus, followed by having Him speaking to you and through you with clarity and passion as well as power and authority.

Response

Notes

NOTE

1. John Gillies, "Editor's Preface," in *Historical Collections of Accounts of Revival* (Edinburgh: Banner of Truth Trust, 1981), vi, http://quintapress.macmate.me/PDF_Books/Historical_Collections_v1.pdf

SECTION EIGHT

THE ALTAR'ED LIFE

The man brought me back to the entrance of the
temple, and I saw water coming out from under
the threshold of the temple toward the east....
The water was coming down from under the
south side of the temple, south of the altar.
—EZEKIEL 47:1

1

UNTIL THE GLORY SHINES THROUGH

Who Himself carried up to the Cross our sins in His body and offered Himself there as on an altar, doing this in order that we, having died to respect to our sins, might live with respect to righteousness (1 Peter 2:24 Wuest).

The ministry of Jesus had reached a critical moment. He had spent almost three years healing the sick, raising the dead, and setting the captives free. But as He climbed the mountain with His three confidants He realized the time had come for Him to focus on His destiny. His destiny was to alter the human race. Offering Himself "as on an altar" would enable those who believed in His Name to die in respect to sin and live in respect to righteousness.

His transfiguration would become a spiritual picture of what it means to live an altar'ed life. Jesus built an altar by being fully and completely given to prayer. Suddenly, a cloud manifested filled with glorious light, holy gladness, and celestial radiance around Him and His disciples. Moses and Elijah appeared and began speaking with Him.

The manifestation of the cloud of glory caused His countenance to be altered and His clothes to both shine as bright as the noon day sun and glisten as freshly fallen snow (see Luke 9:29). The disciples noticed the light was not being shone upon Him from without, but glorious light shone out of Him from within. He was completely irradiated. His Person blazed in celestial glory. What a contrast to Isaiah 52:14, which prophetically declared that at the Cross, "his appearance was so disfigured beyond that of any man and his form marred beyond human likeness."

The Lord's transfiguration was an expansion of Moses' experience on Mount Sinai and a precursor to His own resurrection. Hundreds of years earlier, Moses climbed up the mountain and was covered by the glory of the Lord. When he returned to Israel's camp his face shone with heavenly light (see Exod. 34:30). Paul said the Israelites could not look steadily at the face of Moses because of the glory, transitory though it was. He tells us that the glory that Moses and Israel experienced has no comparison with the surpassing glory that we experience. "And if what was fading away came with glory, how much greater is the glory of that which lasts!" (2 Cor. 3:7-11).

What makes the ministry of the Spirit so glorious? Because of the work of Jesus Christ on the Cross, we are now dead in respect to sin and alive in respect to righteousness. In other words, if we could "see" into the realm of the Spirit, we would "see" righteousness shining out from us. We have been given the Spirit of the Lord, and where the Spirit of the Lord is there is freedom, liberty, and glory. Embracing the altar'ed life transforms and changes us into His image with ever-increasing glory, which comes from the Lord who is the Spirit (see 2 Cor. 3:16-18).

Reflection

When an old pair of jeans becomes really worn around the knees, holes develop in the material exposing the skin beneath. The holes cause the skin to "show through." In a similar way as our altar'ed life develops and becomes our way of life, the inward life of the Holy Spirit will begin to shine through. The flesh (we live in) then wears thin, and the righteousness (light) of God shines outward revealing the glory of God. Every experience we have of His manifested glory is changing us into His image and transforming us from glory to glory by the Spirit of the Lord (see 2 Cor. 3:18).

Response

2

SEATED WITH HIM

And God raised us up with Christ and seated us with him in the heavenly realms in Christ Jesus (Ephesians 2:6).

Every experience in the altar'ed life must be Christ-centric. The Lord Jesus Christ must have preeminence (see Col. 1:18). He is the One to be lifted high, chief and absolute. The Father raised Christ from the dead and "seated him at his right hand in the heavenly realms, far above all rule and authority, power and dominion, and every title that can be given, not only in the present age but also in the one to come." God placed all things under the feet of Jesus, "and appointed him to be head over everything for the church, which is his body" (Eph. 1:20-23).

Jesus Christ "is the very One Who ascended higher than all the heavens, in order to fill the whole universe" (Eph. 4:10). The Greek word for "ascend" is *anabaino*. This compound of *ana* (up) and *basis* (to walk, a pace, a base, the foot) means, "to go up, to rise, to mount,

229

to be borne up, to spring up." Thus to *ascend* is *to walk or step up.*[1] The life of the Lord Jesus Christ is the way of life in the heavenly realms and is far above all else.

Because we are "in Him" we can live from above, overcoming the darkness and the circumstances of life. Jesus Christ is the Ascended One! Being seated with Him means we can live an ascended life. I am not speaking of the previous order, when people were striving to find victory. Living a victorious life does not have to be put off into the future.[2] His intent is that now, through the church, "the manifold wisdom of God should be made known to the rulers and authorities in the heavenly realms, according to his eternal purpose which he accomplished in Christ Jesus" (Eph. 3:10-11).

Living an altar'ed life makes us aware that we have died with Him, risen with Him, and ascended with Him. From there we begin to see everything and everyone differently. His manifested Presence enables us to see from the Lord's point of view. Examples include Isaiah, who saw the Lord seated on a throne, high and exalted, and the train of His robe filled the temple, and John who had a similar experience on the Isle of Patmos (see Isa. 6:1-8; Rev. 1:13). The *train of His robe* Isaiah saw and *the golden sash* in John's vision both speak to the Lord's glory, power, and provision.

From heavenly places we can see the Lord Jesus Christ has been appointed heir of all things (see Heb. 1:2). He has been given all authority, glory, and power. "The Spirit testifies with our spirit that we are God's children. If we are children, then we are heirs—heirs of God and co-heirs with Christ" (Rom. 8:16-17). We have been given full access as joint heirs with Him, or as Paul said He "blessed us in the heavenly realms with every spiritual blessing in Christ" (Eph. 1:3).

Our altar'ed way of life must break out of the four walls of the modern church and into the lives of others. We must speak out of who we are in Christ Jesus, not just what we have learned. We must walk in the newness of the ascended life. We have been planted together in the likeness of His death, raised in the likeness of His resurrection, and seated with Him far above all principalities and powers (see Rom. 6:4-5).

Reflection

The marks of an altar'ed life are consistency, faithfulness, and stability. The fire that originally came from above and must never go out on the altar (see Lev. 6:12-13). Take time today to fan the flame. Ask the Lord to help you see from His perspective as you worship and adore His holy Name.

Response

NOTES

1. Strong, *Strong's Exhaustive Concordance*, G305.
2. Kelley Varner, *Secrets of the Ascended Life* (Shippensburg, PA: Destiny Image Publishers, 2006), 28.

3

THE PRIZE OF THE HIGH CALLING OF GOD

I press toward the mark for the prize of the high calling of God in Christ Jesus (Philippians 3:14 KJV).

In Paul's letter to the Philippians he speaks of his altar'ed life like that of a marathon runner. His words speak to the fact of him having a powerful and glorious conversion. Yet as powerful and glorious as it was, there was more. The "more" was *the prize of the high calling*. Paul had made great progress in Christlikeness. He had been seated with Christ in heavenly places (see Eph. 1:3). The life he lived in the body, he had learned to live by faith in the Son of God (see Gal. 2:20). Paul had set his mind on things above, not on earthly things (see Col. 3:2). But the goal of being "perfect" was still before him, not behind him. His commitment to "press on" tells us that he was not discouraged, but encouraged and willing to continue his pursuit because of the high calling set before him.[1]

Like Paul, our pursuit demands that we forget the things that are behind us. This idea speaks of two things: 1) our old, pre-Christian life and 2) our previous progress as a Christian.

For some people this is a difficult thing. Some have lived a horrible life before coming to Christ while others have struggled to follow Him. Either way, the best way of forgetting is stretching forward (*epekteinomenos*). Like a runner leaning forward at the tape, the more focused one is on the tape, the easier it is to *forget the things behind.*

Paul was focused on the high calling. He saw himself exerting all his strength and pressing on with intense concentration in order not to fall short of the goal that Christ had set for his life—Paul's oneness with Christ.[2]

The high calling cries for us to live above the lower realms. We cannot be focused on all the stuff (cares of life and deceitfulness of riches) or junk (lust of the flesh, lust of the eyes, and the pride of life). We are essentially spirit, not earth dust. We should not be human beings trying to have a spiritual experience, but rather spirits who have been raised to new life in Christ Jesus by the power of the Holy Spirit. We should stop trying to "fit" and seek to be "full." Paul said:

> *You have been raised with Christ, set your hearts on things above, where Christ is seated at the right hand of God. ... Put to death, therefore, whatever belongs to your earthly nature...and put on the new self, which is being renewed in knowledge in the image of its Creator* (Colossians 3:1,5,10).

We are to stay focused on Jesus (the Author and Finisher of our faith) as we run (see Heb. 12:2). The goal of being one with Christ continually moves before us as we press on, and yet that goal is never out of sight. Such should be the mentality of all spiritual adults. We must:

Do nothing out of selfish ambition or vain conceit, but in humility consider others better than yourselves. Each of you should look not only to your own interests, but also to the interests of others. Your attitude should be the same as that of Christ Jesus (Philippians 2:3-5).

Reflection

Such resolve is necessary for us to live an altar'ed life. Throughout our lives all kinds of distractions and temptations such as worry, fear, riches, and unbelief threaten to move our focus away from and choke off our commitment to the Lord Jesus. We must order our thoughts and conversation with things that are true, noble, right, pure, lovely, excellent, and praiseworthy (see Phil. 4:8). Keep your eyes on the Lord Jesus as the Source and Goal of your life.

Response

NOTES

1. Robertson, "Commentary on Philippians 3:12," *Robertson's Word Pictures of the New Testament*, http://www.biblestudytools .com/commentaries/robertsons-word-pictures/philippians/ philippians-3-12.html.

2. Donald C. Stamps and J. Wesley. Adams, *Life in the Spirit Study Bible* (Grand Rapids, MI: Zondervan, 2003).

4

THE FULLNESS OF THE SPIRIT

And be not drunk with wine, wherein is excess; but be filled with the Spirit (Ephesians 5:18 KJV).

The Holy Spirit is not a substance. We must not think of Him as wind, breath, oil, or water. Therefore, we must not think of the Holy Spirit filling our hearts as we would think of water filling a bottle, a vacuum, or an empty basket. The heart of the believer is not a receptacle to be emptied in order that the Holy Spirit might fill it. The Holy Spirit is a Person, and when a believer is full of the Spirit that believer is led, guided, and controlled by the Spirit.[1]

The expression, "filled with the Spirit" speaks of the Spirit possessing the heart and soul of the believer. This possession implies His control over that person's mind and heart.[2] Thus the words *full* and *filled* refer to the control the Spirit exerts over the believer who is said to be filled with Him. The Spirit's fullness brings the believer to the place of obedience and conformity to the Word and the will of God. Therefore, when we speak of a Christian being filled with the Spirit, we are referring to the control that a divine Person, the Holy Spirit, has over a human being, a believer.[3]

On the Day of Pentecost in Acts 2, believers were filled with the Holy Spirit and began speaking languages or tongues as the Spirit enabled them. Later, after the Church gathered for prayer due to the threats of the Sanhedrin, believers were filled with the Holy Spirit and spoke the word of God boldly. In each of these instances the fullness of the Spirit resulted in the believers submitting to the Spirit's control and the Spirit manifesting His Presence.

Paul commands the Ephesian believers to be full of the Spirit instead of being in a state of intoxication with wine. The very fact that they were exhorted to do something means that the action of them being filled would be the result of them making the decision to be filled. This tells us that the believer is not controlled by the Spirit because the Spirit indwells him.[4] The believer must consciously submit and yield to the Holy Spirit continually.

The results of "being filled with the Holy Spirit" begin with the Spirit breaking the power of the sin nature, followed by the isolation and suppression of that nature. This is followed by the person living by the guidance and sustaining energy of the Spirit resulting in the development of the fruit of the Spirit and a desire for the gifts of the Spirit (see Gal. 5:22-23; 1 Cor. 14:1).

Reflection

> The workings of the Holy Spirit are invisible, glorious, and gentle, and within them, He never tells us about Himself. He comes to glorify Jesus—helping us to see Jesus more, to understand Jesus better, to respond to Jesus more obediently, and to love Jesus with a deeper heart of commitment.[5]

The Holy Spirit comes to penetrate us, which is in reality the invisible penetrating the visible. How does the Holy Spirit do this? Our sensitive submission to the Holy Spirit results in:

- He (the Holy Spirit) guiding us into all Truth (Christ Jesus) (John 16:13)

- He quickening and convincing us (Rom. 8:11-16)

- He revealing the deep things of God (1 Cor. 2:10)

- He empowering us to witness (Acts 1:8)

- He praying for and through us (Jude 1:20; Rom. 8:26)

- He producing fruit through our lives (Gal. 5:22-23)

- He administrating His gifts (1 Cor. 12:1-28)

- He giving righteousness, peace, and joy (Rom. 14:17)

Response

NOTES

1. Kenneth S. Wuest, *Untranslatable Riches from the Greek New Testament* (William B. Eerdmans Pub., 1942), 103.

2. Joseph Henry Thayer and James Strong, *A Greek–English Lexicon of the New Testament* (Grand Rapids: Baker Book House, 1977), Strong's G4137, https://www.blueletterbible.org/lang/lexicon/lexicon.cfm?Strongs=G4137&t=KJV.

3. Wuest, *Untranslatable Riches from the Greek New Testament*, 103.

4. Ibid.

5. Jack Hayford, "Symbols of the Holy Spirit," Jack Hayford Ministries, accessed September 29, 2016, http://www.jackhayford.org/teaching/articles/symbols-of-the-holy-spirit/.

5

PRAY IN THE SPIRIT ON ALL OCCASIONS

And pray in the Spirit on all occasions with all kinds of prayers and requests. With this in mind, be alert and always keep on praying for all the saints (Ephesians 6:18).

We have learned that the altar was first a place where stones were piled, where wood was laid, and a sacrifice was offered. The Lord Jesus Christ laid down His life on the Cross as the supreme sacrifice thus becoming an altar'ed Person. Now, as altar'ed people it is important for us to pray in the Spirit on all occasions.

Praying in the Spirit can include the Holy Spirit interceding for us, the Holy Spirit enabling us, or the Holy Spirit speaking from us. Sometimes He prays with groans that words cannot express (see Rom. 8:26-27). At other times He gives the utterance or ability to pray in an unknown language or tongue (see Acts 1:4). Praying in the Spirit will always build a believer up in their most holy faith (see Jude 1:20).

Praying in the Spirit is the last piece of the armor of God listed by Paul in his Ephesian letter. Each of us must stand against the devil's schemes. Our struggle is not against flesh and blood, but against the rulers, against the authorities, against the powers of this dark world and against the spiritual forces of evil in the heavenly realms. Along with the belt of truth, the breastplate of righteousness, the readiness that comes from the Gospel of peace and the shield of faith, we must take up the helmet of salvation and the sword of the Spirit, which is the Word of God. Praying in the Spirit enables us to evaluate and determine satan's line of attack as well as enabling us to stand against all assaults (see Eph. 6:10-18).

The Spirit enables us because He knows what we ought to pray for. He searches our hearts and knows the mind of God because the Spirit intercedes for the saints in accordance with God's will (see Rom. 8:26-27). Each activity is performed by the power and enabling of the Holy Spirit. In the most practical terms it means that the Holy Spirit inspires, guides, energizes, and sustains our praying. Paul prayed that the God of our Lord Jesus Christ would give us the Spirit of wisdom and of revelation in the knowledge of Him, having the eyes of our hearts enlightened so that we may know what is the hope to which he has called us, the riches of his glorious inheritance in the saints, and the immeasurable greatness of his power toward us who believe (see Eph. 1:15-19). Mike Bickle says:

> There is a dynamic relationship between our lifestyle and our ability to enjoy prayer. Our spiritual capacity to experience and enjoy God increases as we walk in purity. ...Where there is ongoing, willful compromise in our lives, it will greatly hinder our spiritual growth and our capacity to agree with God in prayer. Sin hinders our love for Him. We must sincerely seek to live in wholehearted

obedience because obedience is not optional in the kingdom life.[1]

Reflection

Praying in the Spirit necessitates a relationship with the Spirit. Our praying relationship cannot be founded on only making requests of Him but on learning His ways. Begin by praying for wisdom and revelation, then pray through a passage of the Bible. Take time for the Spirit to emphasize or illuminate a word or phrase. Concentrate on what He is revealing and pray accordingly. Ask Him to pray through you. Open yourself to His leading, His language, and His Presence. Wait on Him. Rest in Him. Pray in the Spirit. Embrace and enjoy, in Jesus' Name. Amen.

Response

NOTE

1. Mike Bickle, "Characteristics of Effective Prayer," IHOPKC Blog, March 3, 2016, http://www.ihopkc.org/resources/blog/characteristics-of-effective-prayer.

6

PRAYING WITH MY SPIRIT AND MIND

I will pray with my spirit, but I will also pray with my mind (1 Corinthians 14:15).

Praying in the Spirit is a supernatural manifestation of the Holy Spirit. Such prayer is Holy Spirit inspired and led. As we learned in our previous lessons, such inspired prayer can be in the language of the speaker or the Spirit praying with groans that words cannot express (see Rom. 8:26-27). At other times the Spirit gives the utterance or ability to pray in an unknown language or tongue (see Acts 2:4). Praying in the Spirit will always build a believer up in their most holy faith (see Jude 1:20).

This type of praying flows from the human spirit that has been made alive and then filled with the Holy Spirit. In the Corinthians' services there were instances of ecstatic praying and singing without intelligent words. The Corinthians who were practicing such praying and singing did not see the value of understanding what they were saying. They were choosing to involve their spirit in their praying but not their understanding, making their minds unfruitful. In other words, because they did not know what they were praying, they did not know what to expect or know when their prayers were being answered.

It is important that when we pray in the Spirit we pray with our spirit and our understanding. A.T. Robertson says, "Paul is distinctly in favor of the use of the intellect in prayer. Prayer is an intelligent exercise."[1] Paul preferred praying and singing that reaches the intellect as well as stirs the emotions. Paul said such praying or singing should be done with the understanding also (*psalô de kai tôi noï*).[2]

> *Prayer in the Spirit is prayer whose supreme object is the glory of God;* only in a secondary sense does it seek a blessing for self or for others. This is not natural to us, for it is our natural tendency to be more concerned with our own interests and glory. The Holy Spirit will help us in this weakness, and will impart the motivation to shift our center from self to God.[3]

Praying from our spirit (first) shifts our prayer life to His Kingdom coming and His will being done (on earth as it is in heaven).

> Samuel Chadwick points out that the Holy Spirit never works alone; His activity is always in cooperation with human beings. "He depends upon human cooperation for the mediation of His mind, the manifestation of His truth, and the effectual working of His will. ...We pray in the Spirit, and the Spirit maketh intercession for us."

> Andrew Murray said, "Just as wonderful and real is the divine work of God on the throne graciously hearing, and by His mighty power, answering prayer. Just as divine as is the work of the Son, interceding and securing

and transmitting the answer from above, is the work of the Holy Spirit in us in the prayer that awaits and obtains the answer. The intercession within is as divine as the intercession above."[4]

Reflection

Samuel M. Zwemer said, "True prayer is God the Holy Spirit talking to God the Father in the Name of God the Son, and the believer's heart is the prayer-room."[5] It is important when the Holy Spirit is speaking that we ask for, desire, and seek after the full understanding of His intercession. Praying in this manner causes us to rejoice evermore, pray without ceasing, and in everything give thanks (see 1 Thess. 5:16-18). Pray with your spirit and your mind also.

Response

NOTES

1. Robertson, "Commentary on 1 Corinthians 14:15," *Robertson's Word Pictures of the New Testament*, http://www.biblestudytools .com/commentaries/robertsons-word-pictures/1-corinthians/1 -corinthians-14-15.html

2. Ibid.

3. J. Oswald Sanders, "Praying in the Spirit," in *Prayer Power Unlimited* (Chicago: Moody Press, 1977), 62. Reprinted by permission.

4. Ibid., 63.

5. Samuel M. Zwemer, *Into All the World* (Grand Rapids, MI: Zondervan Pub. House, 1943), 160.

7

LIVING AND WALKING IN THE SPIRIT

Since we live by the Spirit, let us keep in step with the Spirit (Galatians 5:25).

The apostle Paul spent much of his time in prison writing to the churches concerning their spiritual lives. He continually indicated that the Presence and activity of the Holy Spirit was essential to the life of the believer. His own testimony indicates that he lived a life under the guidance and sustaining energy of the Holy Spirit.[1] He wrote to the Romans, "Those who live according to the sinful nature have their minds set on what that nature desires; but those who live in accordance with the Spirit have their minds set on what the Spirit desires...the mind controlled by the Spirit is life and peace" (Rom. 8:5-6).

Paul spoke to them in several different ways that it was important for them to be under the influence of the Holy Spirit. He told

247

them that the Spirit would help them to pray (see Rom. 8:26). "The kingdom of God is...righteousness, peace and joy in the Holy Spirit" (Rom. 14:17). As Christians, it was God's will for them to abound in hope through the Holy Spirit (see Rom. 15:13). He also wrote to the Galatians, "The fruit of the Spirit is love, joy, peace, patience, kindness, goodness, faithfulness, gentleness and self-control" (Gal. 5:22-23).

"When the flesh is represented as lusting against the Spirit, however, it seems equivalent to the 'carnal mind,' i.e. the mind of the sinful natural man as distinct from the mind of the spiritual man."[2] Living in the Spirit increases one's understanding that we have not received the spirit of the world but the Spirit who is from God (see 1 Cor. 2:12).

Walking in the Spirit occurs as we make our steps by the help, guidance, and Presence of the Holy Spirit. Paul and those he traveled with were continually conscious of the Spirit's Presence, power, and guidance.

> The Holy Spirit is represented as animating this body [of Christ], as communicating to it life, and directing all its affairs. ...In the body of believers the Spirit is the sovereign energy which rules completely. By one Spirit all are baptized into one body and made to drink of one Spirit (1 Cor. 12:13). All the gifts of the church, charismatic and otherwise, are from and by the Spirit (1 Cor. 12:4,8-11; Rom. 12:4-8). ...The church is the habitation of the Spirit (Eph. 2:22). ...Thus, the whole life of the church falls under the operation of the Holy Spirit.[3]

Living and walking in the Spirit causes us to represent Christ to others. Paul told the Thessalonians:

> *Make it your ambition to lead a quiet life, to mind your own business and to work with your hands, just as we told*

you, so that your daily life may win the respect of outsiders and so that you will not be dependent on anybody (1 Thessalonians 4:11-12).

Reflection

Living and walking in the Spirit calls for us to live and walk circumspectly, not as unwise but as wise, and making the most of every opportunity, because the days are evil. This means we live and walk with watchfulness in every way and with attention to guard against surprise or danger. The form of the Holy Spirit living through us is chiefly supernatural; that is, the miraculous endowment of His Presence gives the power and wisdom for extending the Kingdom of God. Determine to live and walk in the Spirit each and every day. Begin each morning with these words, "Order my steps today, in everything I do and say."

Response

NOTES

1. Orr, *International Standard Bible Encyclopedia,* s.v. "Holy Spirit, 2," http://www.internationalstandardbible.com/H/holy-spirit-2.html.

2. Ibid.

3. Ibid.

APPLICATION

And in him you too are being built together to become a dwelling in which God lives by his Spirit (Ephesians 2:22).

Throughout this book I have been accentuating the alteration that happens to a person who encounters, embraces, and enjoys the altar of His Presence. The altar'ed life is filled with progressive understanding. God's Word and Spirit are always proceeding into our lives. No Christian should confine himself to a spiritual life within the boundaries of the walls of traditional beliefs and standardized theologies. We must not limit the operation or administration of the Holy Spirit. As Christians we are admonished to grow in the grace and knowledge of the Son of God. We are to speak the truth in love, so we will in all things grow up into Him who is the Head, that is, Christ. We are instructed to integrate the mysteries the Holy Spirit reveals to us until we all reach unity in the faith and in the knowledge of the Son of God and become mature (see Eph. 4:11-16).

251

Reflection

The Holy Spirit should be filling your life and flowing freely out of your innermost being (see John 7:37-39). His glorious revelation of the heavenly Father and the Lord Jesus Christ "should be changing your way of life and revealing the Lord's goodness, grace, and glory to everyone you meet.

J. Stuart Holden said, "Here is the secret of prevailing prayer, to pray under a direct inspiration of the Holy Spirit, whose petitions for us and through us are always according to the Divine purpose, and hence certain of answer." Pray in the Holy Spirit each day. Such praying is but cooperating with the will of God, and such prayer is always victorious.

There are many believers who say prayers but do not pray. They seek God's assistance without the thought of them deepening their relationship with Him. The only secret of a real prayer life is "be filled with the Spirit" who is "the Spirit of grace and supplication" (Eph. 5:18; Zech. 12:10). The very same Spirit who raised Christ from the dead is given to every man in Christ Jesus. In other words, there are no heavenly resources given that have not been made available to you.

Embrace the full nature of Christ Jesus. Your oneness with Christ will manifest His goodness, grace, and glory. He will show you the ways of divine cooperation in service and in the manifestation of the Presence of God. The altar'ed life is His life. Make yourself available to the Holy Spirit, for He is Spirit and life! Resolve today to walk the paths of complete obedience. Throw open the gates of your mind to the Word of the Lord. Open your ears and hear what the Spirit is saying today. Give your heavenly Father, Savior, and Wonderful Counselor the opportunity to speak to your listening ear.

Through the Day

His divine power has given us everything we need for life and godliness through our knowledge of him who called us by his own glory and goodness. Through these he has given us his very great and precious promises, so that through them you may participate in the divine nature and escape the corruption in the world caused by evil desires. For this very reason, make every effort to add to your faith goodness; and to goodness, knowledge; and to knowledge, self-control; and to self-control, perseverance; and to perseverance, godliness; and to godliness, brotherly kindness; and to brotherly kindness, love. For if you possess these qualities in increasing measure, they will keep you from being ineffective and unproductive in your knowledge of our Lord Jesus Christ. (2 Peter 1:3-8).

Response

Notes

Conclusion

HIS ABIDING PRESENCE

And this is his command: to believe in the name of his Son, Jesus Christ, and to love one another as he commanded us. Those who obey his commands live in him, and he in them. And this is how we know that he lives in us: We know it by the Spirit he gave us (1 John 3:23-24).

I pray this study of the altar of His Presence brought you in contact with the manifest Presence of God. Your experience is no doubt different than that of others and yet similar. In the Old Testament the manifest Presence of Yahweh was known as Shekinah. The Shekinah is described in *The 1901 Jewish Encyclopedia* as "the majestic presence or manifestation of God which has descended to 'dwell' among men."[1]

The Shekinah has historically manifested as a cloud. Such is seen in 1 Kings 8:10-11, which says, "And it came to pass, when the priests were come out of the holy place, that the cloud filled the house of the Lord, so that the priests could not stand to minister because of the cloud: for the glory of the Lord had filled the house of the Lord" (KJV). In our natural world:

> Clouds are visible accumulations of tiny water droplets or ice crystals in the Earth's atmosphere. ...Clouds usually appear white because the tiny water droplets inside them are tightly packed, reflecting most of the sunlight that hits them. White is how our eyes perceive all wavelengths of sunlight mixed together. ...Clouds form when air becomes saturated, or filled, with water vapor.[2]

The metaphoric and symbolic uses of clouds in Scripture are many and provide some of the most powerful and glorious illustrations. English Baptist pastor and biblical scholar John Gill wrote that Isaiah 60:8, "Who are these that fly as a cloud, and as the doves to their windows?" (KJV) is:

> Referring to the vast number of converts...who are being compared to a 'cloud' for the number of them, covering Judea as the clouds do the heavens; and for their elevation and situation, being raised from an earthly to a heavenly state; called with a high calling, and made partakers of an heavenly one; and for their being filled with the grace of God, as clouds with water; and for their unanimity, their coming together in a body, making as it were one cloud, and that openly and publicly, professing Christ, and joining them to his church.[3]

> *So Moses went out and told the people what the Lord had said. He brought together seventy of their elders and had them stand around the Tent. Then the Lord came down in the cloud and spoke with him, and he took of the Spirit that was on him and put the Spirit on the seventy elders. When*

the Spirit rested on them, they prophesied, but they did not do so again (Numbers 11:24-25).

Clouds, according to McKenzie, are "an almost universal element of the theophany." The occurrences of clouds indicating the Divine presence are heavily distributed throughout both Testaments. The cloud is, perhaps, the earliest element that was connected to the Divine Presence by Israel. The "Pillar of Cloud" guided and protected the Israelites during their escape. The Israelites first met [the Lord], at the foot of Mt. Sinai, when the mountain was covered in a cloud (Exodus 19:16).

Hiebert suggests that the image of the cloud is connected to the Hebrew term for "glory." While this image is directly connected to Priestly writings and, often, associated with the Temple, Hiebert argues that it "may more narrowly also derive from the aura of the fiery storm cloud."

The Hebrew word for cloud...is `anan. This term denotes a cloud mass, or fog. The term can also connote a collection of clouds. The term is theological and was distinguished from the term denoting the individual contoured storm cloud, a meteorological event which brings rain, "`ab." It is theologically significant to recognize that the cloud mass or collection is complete. It fully hides [the Lord] from the view of the people. This is in keeping with the ancient Israelite mentality that thought that to see God meant death (Judges 13:22, etc.). In other words, as [the Lord] approaches the heavy clouds collect and shield the people from seeing his glory. His presence is signified by the heavy cloud mass or deck which reflects His all-encompassing and, possibly, overwhelming power.[5]

In the New Testament, the Lord's cloud of glory appeared on and around Jesus on the Mount of Transfiguration. Mark 9:2-8 says:

> *After six days Jesus took Peter, James and John with him and led them up a high mountain, where they were all alone. There he was transfigured before them. His clothes became dazzling white, whiter than anyone in the world could bleach them. And there appeared before them Elijah and Moses, who were talking with Jesus. Peter said to Jesus, "Rabbi, it is good for us to be here. Let us put up three shelters—one for you, one for Moses and one for Elijah." **Then a cloud appeared and enveloped them**, and a voice came from the cloud: "This is my Son, whom I love. Listen to him!" Suddenly, when they looked around, they no longer saw anyone with them except Jesus.*

In Acts 1:9 the Shekinah appeared again. As Jesus was taken up before the very eyes of His apostles, a cloud hid Him from their sight. His ascension took place as the Lord Jesus Christ entered into and was carried away in a cloud. There is no mention of the Shekinah appearing in theophanic form after the ascension of the Lord Jesus. No doubt the reason is that we believers are now the temple, the dwelling place, the place of habitation for the Holy Spirit and the glory of God.

First Corinthians 6:19-20 says, "Do you not know that your body is a temple of the Holy Spirit, who is in you, whom you have received from God? You are not your own; you were bought at a price. Therefore, honor God with your body." Paul continues his same thought in 2 Corinthians 6:16 with, "What agreement is there between the temple of God and idols? For we are the temple of the living God."

When the "cloud of His Presence" fills our lives to the point that we are full of the Lord's "reign," streams of living water will flow from us (see John 7:38-39). Our living in the altar of His Presence should inspire others to choose to abide in and foster the Master's manifested Presence. Together we make up the Lord's Shekinah. It is the Lord's Shekinah filling, consuming, consecrating, and manifesting through our thoughts, words, actions, and lives that we must seek in this modern age.

First Thessalonians 3:13 says, "May he strengthen your hearts so that you will be blameless and holy in the presence of our God and Father when our Lord Jesus comes with all his holy ones." When we build an altar by entering His gates with thanksgiving—the Lord meets us there. When we build an altar by praying together in the Spirit—the Lord meets us there. The Lord Jesus Christ comes in the glory He asked the Heavenly Father for in John 17.

> *My prayer is not for them alone. I pray also for those who will believe in me through their message, that all of them may be one, Father, just as you are in me and I am in you. May they also be in us so that the world may believe that you have sent me. I have given them the glory that you gave me, that they may be one as we are one: I in them and you in me. May they be brought to complete unity to let the world know that you sent me and have loved them even as you have loved me. Father, I want those you have given me to be with me where I am, and to see my glory, the glory you have given me because you loved me before the creation of the world* (John 17:20-24).

His glorious Presence is manifested in a much higher degree when a group of believers come together to worship or pray. Such occurred on the Day of Pentecost, during the prayer meeting in Acts 4, and at the house of Cornelius in Acts 10:44-47:

> *While Peter was still speaking these words, the Holy Spirit came on all who heard the message. The circumcised believers who had come with Peter were astonished that the gift of the Holy Spirit had been poured out even on the Gentiles.*

For they heard them speaking in tongues and praising God. Then Peter said, "Can anyone keep these people from being baptized with water? They have received the Holy Spirit just as we have."

Believers are like clouds filled with the Shekinah. We are dust particles connected to the moisture or life of the Spirit. We both reflect and shine the "light of the world."

Jesus said to the people, "I am the light of the world" (John 8:12). He also told those in Matthew 5, "You are the light of the world" (Matt. 5:14). The light of the righteous shines brightly, and the light is the knowledge of the glory of God in the face of Christ (see Prov. 13:9; 2 Cor. 4:6).

Living in the altar of His Presence should bring to light the understanding that believers are like the clouds described in the following Scripture.

His Covenant Is in the Clouds

I have set my rainbow in the clouds, and it will be the sign of the covenant between me and the earth. Whenever I bring clouds over the earth and the rainbow appears in the clouds (Genesis 9:13-14).

His Glory Appears in the Clouds

While Aaron was speaking to the whole Israelite community, they looked toward the desert, and there was the glory of the Lord appearing in the cloud (Exodus 16:10).

The Lord Speaks Out of Clouds

For six days the cloud covered the mountain, and on the seventh day the Lord called to Moses from within the cloud (Exodus 24:16).

His Faithfulness Reaches to the Clouds

Thy mercy, O Lord, is in the heavens; and thy faithfulness reacheth unto the clouds (Psalm 36:5 KJV).

His Truth Is in the Clouds

For thy mercy is great unto the heavens, and thy truth unto the clouds (Psalm 57:10 KJV).

His Strength Is in the Clouds

Ascribe ye strength unto God: his excellency is over Israel, and his strength is in the clouds (Psalm 68:34 KJV).

He Makes the Clouds His Chariot

He wraps himself in light as with a garment; he stretches out the heavens like a tent and lays the beams of his upper chambers on their waters. He makes the clouds his chariot and rides on the wings of the wind (Psalm 104:2-3).

The Lord Rides on Clouds

See, the Lord rides on a swift cloud and is coming to Egypt. The idols of Egypt tremble before him, and the hearts of the Egyptians melt within them (Isaiah 19:1).

The Lord Rises Up as Clouds

Behold, he shall come up as clouds, and his chariots shall be as a whirlwind: his horses are swifter than eagles (Jeremiah 4:13 KJV).

The Lord Comes in the Clouds

At that time the sign of the Son of Man will appear in the sky, and all the nations of the earth will mourn. They will see the Son of Man coming on the clouds of the sky, with power and great glory (Matthew 24:30).

The Lord Comes with Clouds

Look, he is coming with the clouds, and every eye will see him, even those who pierced him; and all the peoples of the earth will mourn because of him. So shall it be! Amen (Revelation 1:7).

The Lord Is Seated upon the Cloud

I looked, and there before me was a white cloud, and seated on the cloud was one "like a son of man" with a crown of gold on his head and a sharp sickle in his hand (Revelation 14:14).

There Are Clouds All Around Us

Therefore, since we are surrounded by such a great cloud of witnesses, let us throw off everything that hinders and the sin that so easily entangles, and let us run with perseverance the race marked out for us (Hebrews 12:1).

I will continue to pray for the Lord to manifest His Presence and glory in your life. I urge you to continue living in the altar of His Presence, to find others who are of a like mind and to become an altar'ed people, who truly abide in His Presence day and night, night and day.

Be joyful always; pray continually; give thanks in all circumstances, for this is God's will for you in Christ Jesus.

Do not put out the Spirit's fire; do not treat prophecies with contempt. Test everything. Hold on to the good. Avoid every kind of evil. May God himself, the God of peace, sanctify you through and through. May your whole spirit, soul and body be kept blameless at the coming of our Lord Jesus Christ. The one who calls you is faithful and he will do it (1 Thessalonians 5:16-24).

We have now come to the end of this book. I pray you have not only embraced the promise of Exodus 30:6, which says, "Put the altar in front of the curtain that is before the ark of the Testimony—before the atonement cover that is over the Testimony—where I will meet with you," but that you have experienced and become the Lord's meeting place. I pray you have become the Lord's trysting place. I pray that you have moved beyond a geographical place or even a place of time reserved for your daily devotions. I pray you now see yourself as His special meeting place. You are that place where the Lord has chosen to abide.

Don't ever wait again to meet the Lord in the sweet bye and bye. Don't settle for the arrival of a church service to start or your favorite minister to call you out and say a special prayer over you. Go now. Meet with the Lord now. Call upon Him now—He is near. He will answer you.

Then I will go to the altar of God, to God, my joy and my delight. I will praise you with the harp, O God, my God (Psalm 43:4).

Do not be carried away by all kinds of strange teachings. It is good for our hearts to be strengthened by grace, not by ceremonial foods, which are of no value to those who eat them. We have an altar from which those who minister at the tabernacle have no right to eat (Hebrews 13:9-10).

Let us now prepare to build us an altar, not for burnt offering, nor for sacrifice: but that it may be a witness between us, and you, and our generations after us, that we might do the service of the Lord (Joshua 22:26-27 KJV).

NOTES

1. Isidore Singer, *The Jewish Encyclopedia* (New York: Funk & Wagnalls Company, 1901), s.v. "Shekinah" http://www .studylight.org/encyclopedias/tje/view.cgi?w=Shekinah.

2. *National Geographic Encyclopedia,* s.v. "Cloud," January 21, 2011, http://nationalgeographic.org/encyclopedia/cloud/.

3. John Gill, "Commentary on Isaiah 60:8," *John Gill's Exposition of the Bible*, http://www.biblestudytools.com/commentaries/gills -exposition-of-the-bible/isaiah-60-8.html.

4. John L. McKenzie, *Dictionary of the Bible* (Milwaukee, WI: Bruce Pub., 1965), 145.

5. John Roskoski, "The Storm-Theophany: A Theology of the Storm" (Paper, St. Peter's College, Middlesex County College), Clouds, http://www.biblicaltheology.com/Research/ RoskoskiJ03.pdf.

ABOUT ROBERT D. STONE

ROBERT D. STONE is an author, minister, and speaker. He and his wife have been involved in full time ministry since 1977. Robert's personal mission is to lead people to a higher dimension of spiritual development and maturity.

Robert continues to travel, teach and encourage others to realize their full potential in Christ Jesus. He desires to write articles, books, and study helps that will live beyond his lifetime as a legacy of his faith in his Lord and Savior, Jesus Christ.

Robert's prayer for you is that you enter, embrace and enjoy an exciting and intimate relationship with the Lord Jesus Christ by the Presence and power of the Holy Spirit. He hopes that you will be changed from faith to faith and glory to glory through the Altar of His Presence.

Robert has been married to the love of his life, Susan, for over forty years. Together they have three children—Talitha, Tanyka, and Tyler.

About His Ministry

For more information about his ministry or materials
you can contact Robert directly by sending an email to him at
robertstone@destinyreformationministries.org
or info@altarofhispresence.com.

Be sure and visit Robert's weekly blog at
https://altaredsite.wordpress.com.

You can also listen to his audio podcast at
http://altarofhispresence.podbean.com.

Also, visit these other websites—

www.bishoprobertstone.com.

www.destinyreformationministries.org.

www.thealtarofhispresence.com.

www.altarofhispresence.com.